# LABOUR-SAVING HINTS
# AND IDEAS FOR THE HOME

# LABOUR-SAVING
# HINTS AND IDEAS
## FOR THE HOME

PRYOR PUBLICATIONS

Re-published by PRIOR PUBLICATIONS © 1991

*Specialists in Facsimile Reproductions*

MEMBER OF
INDEPENDENT PUBLISHERS GUILD

75 Dargate Road, Yorkletts, Whitstable,
Kent CT5 3AE, England.
Telephone & Fax: (01227) 274655
Email: alan@pryor-publish.clara.net
http://home.clara.net/pryor-publish
Kent Exporter of the Year Awards Wiinner 1998

ISBN 0 946014 11 6

*First published by George Routledge & Sons Ltd, November 1924*
*Reprinted December 1924*
*Reprinted January 1925*
*Reprinted July 1992*
*Reprinted December 1997*
*Reprinted May 1998*
*Reprinted September 1998*
*Reprinted August 1999*

# MPG

Printed and bound in Great Britain by
MPG Books Ltd, Bodmin, Cornwall

# PREFACE

THE Hints and Ideas contained in this book are selected from no less than 30,000 entries that were submitted in connection with The Good Housewife Competition, conducted by Messrs. Fleming & Whitelaw, of Australia House, London

So great was the response to the press announcements concerning this Labour Saving in the Home Competition that it was found necessary to discontinue the advertisements after the lapse of a fortnight.

Many of these hints are not wholly confined to labour-saving, but the vast majority of them will be found instructive and interesting.

As the book is intended primarily for reference purposes, a copious index is provided ; but the reader will find entertaining information on any page he or she happens to open.

The Hints and Ideas are published as far as possible in the precise language originally written, so as to preserve intact the spirit of homeliness and open-hearted simplicity which is so often spoiled in editorial hands by a too fastidious regard for grammatical accuracy. Consequently, wherever a hint contains the name of a manufacturer or of his product no attempt has been made to alter it. Naturally, in view of the Competition, Preservene has been recommended by many contributors. No doubt there are many other articles equally deserving of mention, but our chief concern is to reveal the real helps to the busy housewife, yielding in our selection to the claims of efficacy and efficiency.

For much valuable advice and many useful suggestions our thanks are due to The Good Housekeeping Institute, 49, Wellington Street, London, W.C.

# LABOUR-SAVING HINTS AND
# IDEAS FOR THE HOME

1. **To Peel Hot Beetroots.**—Plunge them into cold water. The skin will then peel off like a glove.

2. **Golden Syrup Hint.**—If golden syrup is required in a cake or pudding, do not weigh it in a cup or basin, just flour your scales well, and pour on the golden syrup. You will find it leaves the scales quite easily.

3. **To Remove Marking Ink from Linen.**—A solution of salts of lemon applied with a camel-hair brush will remove marking ink from linen.

4. **To Banish Mice.**—A good way to get rid of mice is to sprinkle oil, or essence, of peppermint about their haunts, and then push a cork firmly into any mouse-hole you may find. Mice have a strong aversion to peppermint, and they cannot nibble through cork.

5. **Window Cleaning.**—Mix equal quantities of water, paraffin and methylated spirit in a bottle ; shake thoroughly and rub on windows and mirrors with newspaper. Polish with an old piece of casement cloth or similar material. This is quite the easiest way of cleaning windows, and the cheapest.

6. **Polishing Linoleum, Surrounds, etc.**—Thoroughly clean linoleum or woodwork with soap, preservene for preference, and warm water. When quite dry paint with Tessaline. This gives a splendid polish and will last for a year or more without another application. This is not

slippery and saves all trouble of polishing and the expense of floor polishes.

7. **To Remove Grease or other Spots from Cloth.**—Preservene soap is wonderful for removing grease or other spots out of woollen materials, such as suits, costumes, etc.

8. **Real Labour Savers.**—To abolish the drudgery of " Brasses " have oak stair rods, enamelled taps, stainless cutlery, tiled or copper curbs, and glass or painted door-knobs, and from half to one hour extra each day is available for recreation.

9. **To Clean Knives.**—Rub hard with a damp dish cloth sprinkled with " Scourine," pressing the knives against the draining-board firmly. This is the quickest and most effective method of removing stains.

10. **Real Labour Savers.**—A good door mat at every door.

11. **To Clean Carpets, Rugs, etc.**—Shred some preservene soap into a saucepan of water ; bring to boil and boil till the liquid is clear. Use very hot on any stains, grease spots, etc., applying with a flannel cloth. When the liquid is cool enough to be borne by hand, wring out flannel in solution and go over whole rug in sections, working first against and then with the grain of rug. Finish each section with a cloth wrung out in clean cold water, and then dry with a cloth that does not leave fluff. Hang rug in air, *not* in the sun, for a time. This treatment revives colour and gives a new lease of life to rugs that receive hard wear.

12. **When Late with the Potatoes** for dinner, before putting them on to boil, cut them the long way instead of across. They will be ready in much less time.

13. **White Enamel Hooks and Taps.**—Paint the hooks and taps in the kitchen, pantry and bath room with white

enamel. It will prevent the towels and cloths getting rust marks when hung up wet. A wipe with a wet cloth rubbed on preservene soap cleans the taps quicker than polishing with metal polish.

14. **To Remove Sewing Machine Oil Stain.**—Yellow stains left by sewing machine oil on white material may be removed by wetting and rubbing with preservene soap before washing.

15. **To Clean Leather Furniture and Suit-cases.**—Wash with suds made of preservene soap and a very little warm water ; rinse off with cold water ; dry it and gloss with the white of an egg. Allow it to dry a little and then polish with a soft duster.

16. **To Clean Ivory Ornaments.**—Rub a wet tooth brush on preservene soap, then on the article to be cleaned. Rinse the ivory in lukewarm water ; dry it and rub with a dry brush until polished.

17. **To Save Hours of Blackleading.**—When the fires are " off," wash down the grates with preservene soap and hot water to take off the old black lead. Dry and apply one or two coats of Japan blacking. When the gloss becomes dim apply black boot polish and rub up with a soft duster.

18. **Try Sweeping the Stairs with a Paint Brush** instead of an ordinary dusting brush, and note the difference. A soft, medium sized paint brush gets into corners and between the rails better than any other.

19. **To Dye a Light Rug a Darker Shade.**—After washing off the dirt with preservene soap, dry it, and get two packets of dye the shade required. Dissolve one packet of dye in a small basin of boiling water, stirring it with a stick until thoroughly dissolved. Take a nail brush ; keep dipping it in the dye and go over the plain surface of the rug,

keeping away from the floral designs. Hang the rug out to dry and next day repeat the process. When dry shake well and brush off the loose dye.

20. **To Clean any kind of Paint.**—Dissolve 4 ozs. of preservene soap in 1½ gallons of hot water. Apply to the paint with a soft rag. A cloth wrung out in clean warm water will fetch all traces of soapy water off the paint, after which a clean duster may be used to give the final polish. This is a very economical and quick way of getting over the worst of the autumn and spring cleaning.

21. **To Clean Silver.**—Take a bar of preservene soap, cut up and add enough hot water to make a jelly. When cold add sufficient powdered whitening to make it the consistency of cream. Put into a covered jar to keep clean. Take a damp flannel, dip in the mixture, and rub the silver. Then rinse well in warm water, wipe quite dry and brighten with a chamois leather, when a most brilliant polish will be produced, leaving no trace of whitening in the crevices.

22. **Easy and Economical Way to Light a Fire.**—Soak a cinder all night in a tin of paraffin. In the morning place the cinder on top of a small piece of paper in the bottom of the grate, cover cinder with small lumps of coal, apply a light to paper, and it will be found that the coal will catch without difficulty from the oil-soaked cinder. A pint of paraffin at the cost of twopence will be sufficient for three fires for a fortnight.

23. **To remove hot dish marks** from a polished table. Simmer a pint of linseed oil for ten minutes then add a quarter-pint of turpentine. Apply this often and rub off with a soft rag.

24. **To Clean Coloured Blinds.**—Rub the faded parts over lightly with linseed oil.

25. **To Clean Linoleum.**—Wash over with warm water and use a little preservene soap to the very dirty parts. Then allow it to dry. Mix a little painters' size with water and rub it lightly over the surface. This makes a lovely polish and will not stick.

26. **Knife Cleaning** can be made much easier by tacking a strip of old carpet tightly on the knife-board and sprinkling with bath brick. This produces a good polish without scraping or wearing out the knife.

27. **To Clean Floor-Polishing Mop.**—In this way, this dirtiest of all articles can be thoroughly cleansed, at a minimum of expense and labour. Soak in strong soda water for twenty-four hours, squeeze and rub well with preservene soap and boil for twenty-four minutes in preservene soapsuds in which clothes have already been boiled. Rinse well.

28. **To roll a Swiss Roll quickly and easily,** turn it out on a wet cloth and just pull up evenly one end of cloth as if tipping the sponge off.

29. **To Pare Young Potatoes or Carrots.**—After being soaked in cold water for fifteen minutes, brush over with a stiff scrubbing brush. This not only removes the skin quickly and easily, but also prevents the hands from becoming stained.

30. **To Clean Windows, Mirrors, Lamp Chimneys, etc.** These should be rubbed with a cotton rag dipped in paraffin, and when nearly dry, polished with soft paper (ordinary newspaper will do). When they will not only be thoroughly clean, but brilliantly polished. By this method a great deal of labour is saved, as they retain their lustre for a long time.

31. **Rinse the Hands in Cold Water after Using Hot Water.**—If you have to wash your hands many times a day, rinse them in cold water after washing in warm. This will close the pores of the skin, and the hands will keep clean much longer. Do not use very hot water as it makes the hands rough and hard. If you use preservene soap your hands will be smooth and soft even in very hard water.

32. **When Boiling Milk.**—You can save time and trouble by putting a large marble into the pan. The marble automatically stirs the milk and prevents it from burning.

33. **Newspapers** can be used for many purposes in the home. If hot liquids are spilt on the stove, a crumpled newspaper will wipe them off without leaving a stain. Windows cleaned with a rag dipped in paraffin and left to dry, then rubbed with a wad of newspaper, will shine and keep clean much longer. If pans are wiped out with a piece of newspaper after frying, and finally with a piece of white paper, they will not burn so easily.

34. **To Remove Tar Marks from White Silk Stockings, Gloves or Clothes.**—Rub well with fresh butter, then wash in a good lather of preservene soap, rinse well and dry.

35. **For Tar Marks on White Shoes** rub with fresh butter, then apply some petrol ; rub well in. Be careful not to apply the petrol when near a fire or light.

36. **Tiles.**—Use a little preservene when cleaning your tiled hall. It will leave a beautiful glossy polish.

37. **Wash Chamois or Gloves in a Lather of Preservene.**— They will remain soft and supple. Do not rinse out the soap, but pat carefully in the folds of a towel ; hang up to dry.

38. **Brown Glacé or Leather Shoes.**—To darken light brown glacé or leather shoes, wipe with a damp flannel

on which you have rubbed a little preservene to remove all dirt and old polish. Then sponge over with liquid ammonia. You will find that they will, when dry, take a beautiful dark polish.

39. **Brasses.**—After cleaning the brasses with ordinary polish, rub a little furniture cream over and polish with a soft cloth. Door knockers, kerbs, etc., will not need cleaning so frequently.

40. **To Remove Paint Stains from Window-panes or Marble** rub well with the edge of a penny, or pencil eraser.

41. **To Remove Stains from White Marble.**—Take 4 ozs. of preservene soap, 1 oz. of soda, 1 oz. of pumice stone powder, 4 ozs. of whitening and half a cake of washing blue. Mix all together with a pint of boiling water. Put into a jar and stand it in a pan of boiling water. Keep it well stirred for twenty minutes, Spread it over the marble while still hot ; leave it for twenty-four hours, then wash off with warm water. Soap, rinse well, and polish with a leather.

42. **To Remove Summer Tan from the Face and Arms** take 1 oz. of Eau de Cologne, 1 oz. of Elder Flower water, 1 oz. of lemon-juice strained through four folds of muslin ; mix together and add drop by drop one teaspoonful of simple tincture of Benzoin. Dab over the skin several times a day.

43. **Camphor Ice.** To make camphor ice for roughened hands, take 2 ozs. each of home-made lard and white wax, and ½ oz. of powdered camphor. Place the wax and lard in a jar ; stand in a saucepan of boiling water ; stir well till melted. Add the powdered camphor and stir till cold ; form into balls and store in a tin. To make home-made lard, procure ¼ lb. of flead from the butcher and run it down in a clean enamelled stew pan.

44. **A Gas Stove Hint.**—Two minutes after lighting the burners in your gas stove, open the oven door for a second or two to allow the moist air to escape and your oven will heat far more quickly after the ventilation.

45. **A Jam Hint.**—Jam which has been laid aside and has got hard and sugary and unfit for use can be made as good as when newly made if it is put into the oven for a little while till the sugar melts and then left to cool.

46. **Fly Stains.**—To prevent flies from marking windows, looking glasses and pictures, clean these with brasso. Only a little is required. It gives a brilliant polish and saves many cleanings when flies are about.

47. **Oil Cloth.**—In a home where there are toddlers, so that it is not safe to polish oilcloth, it is a good plan (after sweeping) to rub the oilcloth vigorously with preservene, using a moist cloth or pad for the purpose. This cleans and polishes at the same time, and also preserves it. Twice a week is sufficient.

48. **Storing Summer Things.**—When putting away summer finery, soak all starched things overnight in cold water to remove the starch. Next day put them in a copper or tin of cold water in which is some shredded preservene soap and also a little blue. Bring slowly to the boil and allow to simmer for half an hour. Rinse first through hot water; then through cold. Dry and air. Put away rough dry (not ironed). When required for use next summer they only require starching and ironing. Dresses, etc., made of ratine, silk, sponge cloth, or any such material, if treated in this way, but not quite boiled, will look quite new next season.

49. **To Clean Plush Upholstered Chairs.**—For cleaning the seats of plush upholstered chairs apply preservene soap with a damp sponge and gently rub well into the material

which is afterwards rinsed by sponging with clean water. It brings up the colour wonderfully.

50.  **An economical Chamois Leather.**—Sew a small one to the centre of a duster, in this way it is all used.  With a big one all the outside edges are crumpled up in the hand.

51.  **To Save Continual Polishing of Linoleum.**—When first laid a coat of clear varnish is carefully applied with a soft brush and allowed to dry thoroughly.  This will retain a brilliant shine and will only need a dry duster or mop to keep clean.  It will also act as a preservative for the linoleum.

52.  **To Impart a Little Stiffness to Sheets** and other articles which ordinarily would not be starched during the wash, but are improved by a slight stiffness, pour a small quantity of starch in the final rinsing or blue water, if used.  The result is a nice finish.

53.  **The Cold Water Method of Washing.**—For those who have no convenience for boiling clothes, the cold water method of using preservene soap will give a result as highly satisfactory as hot.  Follow the directions on the wrapper, and then add a small quantity of " Milton."  Leave for some hours or overnight and rinse well in warm water, and you will be surprised how quickly dirt vanishes even from very soiled parts.  No blueing is required and the result will be the cleanest and whitest linen, equal in colour to any laundry.

54.  **An Ingenious Device.**—Articles drawn up either by tape or elastic are usually tiresome to wash.  Either the tape must be taken out and replaced each time, or else it " runs in."  This is easily obviated by putting a small safety pin at each end, the article can then be drawn at

full length to iron and the pins will serve as a bodkin to
draw tape as required.

55. **A Gas-Stove Hint.**—After black-leading and polishing
a gas cooking stove, give a coat of wax polish. It will
not require any further blacking again for several weeks,
only polishing with a duster.

56. **To Whiten Piano Keys.**—To whiten stained piano
keys make a paste from whitening and solution of potash.
Spread it on and allow it to remain for twenty-four hours,
and the ivories will be restored nearly, if not quite, to their
original colour.

57. **To Clean Dark Furs.**—Heat a quantity of bran in a
pan, taking care not to burn it. When well heated, rub
it thoroughly into the fur. Repeat two or three times.
Shake the fur, and brush until free from dust.

58. **An Economical Floor Cleaner.**—Wash floor well with
warm water and preservene soap to remove stains, etc.,
and when thoroughly dry rub tiles or linoleum with a
paraffin cloth. Polish with a dry mop and floor will keep
clean and bright for weeks, with a daily dust mop.

59. **To Keep Polished Stoves in Good Condition Without
Using Blacklead.**—Oil the parts of the stove with good salad
oil, dust over it some unslacked lime from a muslin bag ;
let it remain a few days. Then rub off with a fine rag.
Polish with a leather. The stove will then be quite smooth
and look like enamel, only needing a daily dusting.

60. **To Make Brass Curtain Poles, etc., Equal to New.**—
Required : preservene soap, 2 oz. oxalic acid (poison), hot
water, soft cotton rags, old nail brush. Method : make
a strong solution of preservene soap by shredding and
boiling in a pan. Brush article all over with this, paying
particular heed to corners, etc. Wash off and if necessary
repeat. Make a strong solution of the oxalic in a saucer.

Apply briskly with a soft cotton rag. Rinse off. Scrub again with preservene solution, rinse, and polish with dry cotton rags. This will produce a finish and sheen like new, and it will last for at least six months. Avoid getting oxalic acid into any cuts on hands, as it is poisonous and painful, though in such small quantities, not dangerous. When all brass is cleaned destroy remainder of oxalic acid by pouring down sink, where it will do good.

61. **A Knitting Hint.**—When knitting stockings and socks, knit mercerised silk or thread with the wool when making heels and toes.

62. **Clothes-line Hint.**—Boil a new clothes line before using it. It will last longer.

63. **Economical Linoleum Cleaner.**—When washing oilcloth and linoleum, add half a cup of ordinary lamp oil to a bucket of water. No scrubbing or polishing is required. This acts as a disinfectant and leaves a shiny surface, thus saving the time of polishing. Specially recommended for the light-coloured, basket-pattern floorings.

64. **Polishing Floors.**—Instead of polishing floors so often, mix together glue and water ; melt down about three-pennyworth of glue, mix with a bucket of warm water. This will polish and keep polished for weeks. Wash the floor as washing with plain water. After this dusting is the only thing needed.

65. **To Full Up Holes in Walls.**—Mix some well broken glass with putty and press mixture well in hole. Finish with putty only. When dry, surface can be painted with surrounding colour.

66. **To Clean Silver in a Hurry.**—Apply methylated spirits with a rag ; let the silver dry for a minute, then

polish with dry soft rag. This is also good for looking glasses.

67. **Preservene Jelly Saves Hours of Labour.**—Dissolve pieces of preservene in a jar, to form a jelly. A little of this jelly added to washing-up water makes china and silver glisten like new. Added to the water used for washing floors, tiles, white paint, etc., scrubbing will be found entirely unnecessary.

68. **To Clean Mirrors.**—Slightly moisten a piece of preservene and then rub it over the mirror, until the surface is well covered. Leave for a quarter of an hour, then rub away the soap with a dry cloth. Finish by polishing with a leather. After this treatment you will find there will be no condensation of moisture.

69. **A Silver Cleaning Hint.**—Wash the silver in a lather of preservene and hot water; dry well, and afterwards polish with a chamois leather. A brilliant polish will soon be obtained.

70. **Greasy Gas Stove.**—When the wash is finished and the clothes removed from the boiler, take the loose parts of the gas stove, oven plates, shelves, etc., brush them to remove loose dirt and put them in the boiler containing the preservene water and boil them for about ten minutes. In the meantime (having taken some of the water for this purpose out of boiler) scrub the immovable parts. Preservene has wonderful properties for dissolving grease and the labour of cleaning the gas stove is reduced to a minimum, and a stove treated thus every fortnight or three weeks will never smell of burnt fat and grease.

71. **A Peg Hint.**—If you haven't a peg apron, made like an exaggerated sewing apron with deep pockets to take the pegs, put your pegs in a shopping bag, slip the handle over the clothes line before you fasten the latter

to the post, then slide the basket along the line ahead of you as you go. When you take in the dry clothes, bring the bag along with you, dropping in the pegs as you go. This saves a lot of stooping and keeps the pegs clean.

72. **To Mend Lace Curtains.**—If torn, wash and iron as usual, then, while the curtain is still lying on the ironing-board, dip a piece of plain net in cold starch, squeeze as dry as possible, lay over the hole, and iron till dry. The edges of the holes should be drawn together as much as possible.

73. **To Clean a Copper Kettle.**—Copper kettles or other utensils that have been dulled or blackened by contact with the fire are easily cleaned by a lemon cut in half, dipped in salt, and rubbed over the surface of the metal, which must be washed afterwards with water to prevent the acid eating into it.

74. **To Clean a Burnt Aluminium Saucepan.**—Pour some water into the pot, and add an onion. Set it on to boil, and very soon all the burnt matter will loosen and rise to the top, leaving the saucepan clean and bright again.

75. **When Woollen Jumpers Need Washing.**—To wash fluffy woollen jumpers, scarves, etc., scald preservene soap shavings and whisk to a thick foam   Add this to luke-warm water along with a teaspoonful of ammonia. Prepare three bowls of water (all exactly the same heat), but the third should be without soap. Squeeze the articles through the first water, work well through the second, and finally rinse in third. Do not pass through a wringer. Squeeze out as much water as you possibly can. Now pin the articles on an old piece of sheet, and hang this out to dry. On no account peg them out, as that would pull them out of shape.

76. **Embroidery Ironing.**—Embroidery requires careful ironing. Fold a blanket three or four times and cover with a clean cloth ; put a thin, damped cloth at the back of the embroidery, and then quickly apply a hot iron on the wet surface until it is quite dry. By this means the pattern of the embroidery will stand out with as good an effect as when new.

77. **To Glaze Linen.**—The articles should first be washed with preservene soap, and dried, after which starch in cold starch and then ironed while still damp. Next, a piece of flannel is dipped in some powdered French chalk and rubbed smoothly over each article, after which a piece of preservene soap is rubbed over the chalk. Finally the articles are ironed on the right side only with a moderately hot iron, and, when finished, this will have the effect of white porcelain, but will in no way injure the article.

78. **To Make Cold Starch.**—$\frac{1}{4}$ lb. of Colman's white starch, 1 teaspoonful of borax, 3 pints of cold water, 1 teaspoonful of turpentine. Hold the starch in the hands under the water and rub perfectly smooth. It is then ready for use.

79. **To Get Up Collars, etc.**—After washing with preservene soap, dip in boiling starch and then dry thoroughly, after which prepare some starch as follows : 2 tablespoonsful of powdered starch, 1 heaped teaspoonful of powdered borax, and 1 teaspoonful of turps or paraffin. Dip in the article, then rub over it a piece of preservene soap, wring out and roll in a clean towel, or put through the wringer. They are now ready to be ironed. Have the irons thoroughly hot, rub over with a piece of preservene soap ; then rub them with a little bathbrick or salt on knifeboard, or thickly folded paper. The result is perfectly clean irons, and the linen beautifully white and stiff, with a good polish as when new. This quantity of starch is sufficient for a dozen fronts and collars.

80. **To Clean Raincoats.**—Shred finely half a cake of preservene soap and dissolve in 1 quart of boiling water. Apply to very soiled and greasy parts of raincoats, and then wash clean with piece of flannel and dry before pressing. Acts like magic.

81. **Furniture Reviver** that removes dirt, grease, stains, etc., and is very cheap. 1 gill each—turpentine, methylated spirits, vinegar and paraffin. Mix well together in a bottle. Shake the bottle well and apply with a soft rag. Polish with soft duster. It produces a splendid polish with very little labour.

82. **To Stop a Leak.**—Make a paste of soap and powdered whiting. This is an excellent temporary stop for a leak.

83. **To Renovate Leather Furniture.**—Wash it with soap and water and when dry apply a little vaseline, rubbed in with the hand. Let it remain until next morning, then polish with a soft duster. This treatment will prevent the leather from cracking.

84. **A Dyeing Hint.**—If you ever have occasion to dye any stockings or socks, always put into the dye as well a small quantity of darning wool. Then when the stocking needs darning you have the wool ready without the difficulty of finding the right shade in the shop.

85. **Use a Grater for Preservene.**—The quickest and best way to shave up preservene is to get an ordinary grater and use your suet side. It is thereby done beautifully fine in a minute and dissolves at once.

86. **Useful Clothes Drier.**—Get an old sunshade or umbrella, strip off cover, enamel white, and hang the handle on a hook in the ceiling, over your cooker or range, and you have a splendid drier or airer, which will hold a large quantity of collars, handkerchiefs and small things on the various wires and points, taking up very little space. It can be closed when not in use.

87. **Linen Gloss Mixture** can be made by dissolving 1 oz. of gum arabic in about half a pint of boiling water. Leave overnight, strain, and put into bottles. Add a teaspoonful of this to each pint of starch used for linen goods.

88. **To Restore Irons.**—Irons lose a good deal of their power to become very hot after having been in use for some years. This is due to the fact that the iron has lost its temper. To remedy this, make the iron as hot as possible, short of red heat, and then carefully put it into a bucket of cold water. Keep the face turned away to avoid any bubbles which may splash up from the water.

89. **To Remove Ink Stains.**—If ink stains in linen are rubbed with ripe tomato they will soon disappear. The linen should then be washed in lukewarm water without soda.

90. **To Wash Blankets.**—Treated in the following way there is no shrinking and blankets last much longer. Put six pennyworth of glue into a jam jar and add a quart of water. Set this in a pot of boiling water and leave until it melts. Pour the solution into a bath of warm water, Place the blankets in the bath, press well down. Leave for half an hour, then swill up and down. Rinse in several clean waters, adding a generous dash of blue to the last. Wring and hang out to dry.

91. **Don't Waste the Odds and Ends of Soap** that are left from the toilet, bath, kitchen and scullery. Shred each piece finely into a 3 lb. jam jar (stone for preference), using one handful of soap to each jar. Add a piece of washing soda the size of a walnut, or, if preferred, a piece of rock ammonia. Fill up the jar with boiling soft water and let it stand till cold, when it will be a thick jelly. A small quantity of this added to the washing-up water or for scrubbing or cleaning paint is most valuable.

92. **To Make Mint Sauce Quickly and Easily.**—Sprinkle the leaves with granulated sugar *before* chopping. You will be delighted with the result.

93. **To Clean White Enamel Baths.**—Wet a cloth with paraffin oil, rub well all round. ' Then take another cloth, which has been rubbed with preservene soap. This will be found to take off all dirt without any injury to the enamel.

94. **To Remove Ink Stains.**—Dip the stained part into cold water, then lay over a board, cover stain with a good layer of common salt ; then squeeze the juice of a lemon over salt, cover over and leave for a couple of hours, after which wash in the usual way.

95. **Clothes Pegs.**—These will last longer if when new they are boiled for ten minutes.

96. **For Removing Shiny Marks from Skirts.**—After having made coffee, pour hot water over the remaining grounds. Dip a cloth in this and rub the shiny parts of dress.

97. **To Clean Brass Candlesticks.**—Wash a greasy candlestick in hot soapy water, lathered with preservene, making sure all candle grease spots are removed. Thoroughly dry, and clean the article with any good metal polish, and polish well with dry whitening. Next smear with a very thin coating of vaseline. This keeps the candlestick bright for several weeks, and further candle-grease spots can be easily removed in the meantime. This method of cleaning applies to all brassware.

98. **Cleaning a Couch or Large Armchair.**—To clean a couch or large armchair, which cannot conveniently be taken out of doors, take a small sheet, large enough to cover right over, and put it in warm water ; then wring as dry as possible. Lay it right over the couch or chair, and beat

thoroughly with a cane or beater.   You will find when you lift the sheet that the dust has risen and stuck to the under side of the damp sheet.

99.  **For Giving Permanent Polish to Linoleum.**—4 ozs. orange shellac dissolved in 1 pint methylated spirits (cost about 2s.), and mixed thoroughly.   Keep covered whilst dissolving, to avoid evaporation.   Thoroughly wash all dirt or dust from floors and then apply solution thinly with wad of linen rag.   The solution dries almost as soon as applied.   This gives a brilliant and permanent polish to the linoleum, thus saving hours of hard work polishing with wax or floor polish, as well as eliminating the continued expense of floor polishes, etc.   The linoleum will then only need dusting with floor mop or duster.

100.  **Paperhanging for Amateurs.**—Amateurs will find wallpaper much easier to hang if they paste the walls instead of the paper.

101.  **Water-bottles, Decanters, etc.,** can easily be cleaned with small pieces of raw potato put into the vessel with equal parts of vinegar and water, and shaken for a few minutes.

102.  **Preservene Soft Soap.**—Procure a tin or jar to hold a quart.   Shred into same one bar of preservene soap. Pour on boiling water till full ; stir till dissolved.   When cold it forms an absolutely perfect soft soap, clean, odourless and economical ; ready for using on floors, baths, sinks, etc., and will not spoil the most delicate hands.   A little paraffin can be added if desired.

103.  **To Chop Up Meat, Vegetables, etc., quickly.**— Instead of using a knife and fork, use two knives, and chop up by keeping the knife blades running alongside each other, but working in opposite directions.

104. **To Remove Hot Dish Marks from Polished Tables.**
—Make a paste of salt and salad oil and coat the marks thickly with this. Leave on an hour or so, and after polishing in the usual way it will be found that all the stains have disappeared.

105. **A Table Wrinkle.**—A piece of zinc, nailed over half of the kitchen table, makes an excellent surface for chopping onions, meat, etc., and can be easily cleaned with a damp cloth.

106. **To Prevent Brass from Tarnishing.**—Heat slightly and paint with a solution made by dissolving half an ounce of shellac in half a pint of methylated spirit. No cleaning will be needed.

107. **Scissors are Very Handy in the Kitchen.**—When using raisins for puddings, mincemeat, etc., which require chopping, try cutting the fruit with the scissors. Scissors can also be used for cutting up candied orange or lemon peel, for cutting the rind from bacon ; also for removing the heads from herrings, sprats, etc.

108. **Boot Polishing Hint.**—Instead of using ordinary boot brushes for cleaning and polishing boots, buy stove brushes instead. These have a handle and can be held firmly, and saves the annoyance of dropping the brushes. Moreover they are cheaper.

109. **To Steam Potatoes Without a Steamer.**—Lay a piece of strong muslin or straining cloth on the kitchen table. On this place the potatoes ; then cover the potatoes with the lid of the saucepan you are using for boiled meat or fruit pudding ; tie the corners of the muslin together across the top of the saucepan lid. Place lid on the saucepan, so that the potatoes are in the muslin between the pudding and the lid. This method saves a saucepan or steamer, also extra fuel.

110. **Sandwich-making Hint.**—When making meat sandwiches for parties, picnics, etc., try adding the mustard to the butter before spreading. This is a quicker method, also the mustard is evenly distributed, instead of being in unpalatable patches.

111. **Blanket Hint.**—To increase the size of blankets which have become shrunk, sew at the sides (if the blankets are too narrow, or at the bottom if too short) a strip of flannelette or calico. This part will do for tucking in at the sides or bottom, as the warmth is required for the covering. This is a good plan for making single bed blankets suitable for a double bed.

112. **Gas Stoves. Aluminium Paint better than Blacklead.**—Perfect cleanliness with much less labour may be obtained by coating the bars and top of a stove front with aluminium paint instead of blacklead, except just over the gas. It will be found quite durable. The top of stove may be wiped clean after use.

113. **Cleaning Knives.**—Before cleaning knives on a knife board, damp them slightly. They clean more quickly and gain a better polish.

114. **To Make a Mangle Last for Years.**—After wringing clothes, get a piece of old blanket and mangle two or three times ; this dries the rollers. When not in use, unscrew and insert two pieces of flat wood at either end of rollers so that a draught may get through.

115. **Hints on Folding.**—When wringing and mangling tablecloths, towels, sheets, etc., fold one week by the hem and next week by selvedge. This makes them wear longer than when always folded in the same manner.

116. **Patent Dress Clips.**—When washing articles with these attached, fasten them securely before putting through the mangle. This keeps them as good as new.

117. **Newspapers.** (1) You can get a better shine on a window by using a newspaper than by any other way. (2) Moths hate the smell of printers' ink and will not come near garments that are covered up with layers of newspapers. (3) Disinfect your galvanised iron dustbins every week by burning two or three newspapers in them, after they have been emptied. This keeps them dry and free from grease.

118. **Cooling Jellies.**—To cool jellies, etc., in short time, take a handful each of salt and soda and put in a bowl of water ; stand jelly mould in it.

119. **Lemons.**—Heat lemons thoroughly before squeezing and you will get nearly double the juice.

120. **Iron Mould Stains.**—Iron mould stains may be quickly removed if the stain is first wetted with cold water and then saturated with this lotion, continually until the stain fades entirely. Mix 1 tablespoonful of lemon-juice, 1 tablespoonful of cream of tartar, and a teaspoonful of oxalic acid in a pint of water.

121. **Stains on Piano Keys.** These stains can be removed if they are ivory keys by rubbing them over with a paste made of whitening and peroxide of hydrogen; after it is brushed off polish with a square of felt.

122. **To Sharpen a Blunt Mincing Machine.**—Grind in it with a piece of bath brick.

123. **Loose Knife Handles.**—Knife tangs which have come away from the handles can be firmly secured again with this simple home-made cement. Mix resin, which has been melted, with a little white sand or brick dust, and fill it into the aperture. Heat the tang, and then press it in securely.

124.  **To Remove the " Fur " from a Kettle.**—A table-spoonful of borax added to a pint of water will remove the fur from a furred kettle if boiled in it.

125.  **Smokeless Wicks.**—A wick soaked in vinegar will never smoke.

126.  **To Keep Flowers Fresh.**—Flowers will keep much longer and last better if their stems are put in lukewarm water to which a saltspoonful of salt has been added.

127.  **To Keep Cheese Fresh.**—The mildew which often forms on cheese can be avoided if a lump of sugar is kept in the cheese dish.

128.  **To Freshen a Much-worn Linoleum.**—New life will be put into linoleum if it is varnished over with a good varnish.   But it should be sparingly used, and not walked upon till quite dry.

129.  **Instead of Chopping or Grating Suet** in the usual way, try this plan.  Take all skin from the suet and sprinkle the pastry-board thickly with flour ;   then roll the suet with the rolling pin until it is flat.  Take it up in floured hands, and it will come apart in small pieces.

130.  **An Inexpensive Knife Cleaner.**—Take a piece of old Brussels carpet, sprinkle it liberally with knife powder, and then fold in two.   Insert the knife and rub vigorously. The result is a brilliant polish in no time, both sides of the knife being cleaned simultaneously.

131.  **Bellows for Dusting.**—When cleaning down, one of the handiest labour-savers is a pair of bellows.   In cleaning the head and foot of a wire spring mattress, where the dust collects, a good pair of bellows blows out the dust and fluff in a minute.   For the back of wardrobes that are too heavy to move, stand at one end and blow the bellows behind along the skirting board, and you will find the dust

out at the other end. For cornices and picture rails, particularly if they are white, dusting often smears them, so take the bellows and blow the dust. Marble clocks with carved columns, heavy bronzes, carved oak, even the type-writer and wireless set all get dusty, but a pair of bellows moves the dust easily, quickly, and without fear of breaking.

132. **Staining Stairs and Floors.**—A very economical and most excellent wearing stain (from experience) is oak solignum. A syrup tin full from your painter and paper-hanger will stain round a decent-sized bedroom floor. The stairs to the top bedrooms or attics look well if solignumed all over—they then need no carpet ; only polish once a week or once a month, and a daily dust or mop. A band about an inch wide, painted black down each side will look like a carpet border, and oak stair rods will give a smart finishing touch.

133. **To Remove Coffee Stains.**—Coffee stains can be entirely removed, even after months, by rubbing in some pure glycerine. Leave this on the stain for half an hour, and then wash with preservene soap.

134. **To Remove Soot Stains from Carpet.**—Cover the stain with salt and brush off with a stiff brush. Repeat the process until stain vanishes. Never wet a soot stain !

135. **To Brown Piecrust.**—When a pie, fruit or other-wise, will not brown nicely on the top, brush the crust lightly with sugar and water, and put it back in the oven. This browns quickly, so keep an eye on it !

136. **An Ironing Hint.**—When ironing a large article, part of it is apt to drag on the floor while you are attending to the other end. To avoid this, use a large ironing sheet, to hang over the side of the table. Pin one end up to form a bag, into which part of the article can fall.

137. **Boiled Bacon.**—To make boiled bacon really delicious, add a teaspoonful of vinegar, two cloves and a little nutmeg to the water. This gives an excellent flavour.

138. **To Renovate Navy Costumes.**—Use a small nail-brush and hot water in which a walnut-sized piece of rock ammonia has been dissolved and the blue-bag has been squeezed until the water is almost the colour of the serge. This, brushed the way of the nap, will improve a dress wonderfully and make it look quite fresh. It should then be ironed, on the wrong side, while still slightly damp.

139. **Rainspots on Felt Hats.**—Remove ribbon or trimmming, then cover the whole hat with pipeclay paste leave this on for a day or two, and brush it off with a stiff brush in the open.

140. **Saving Gas.**—See that the main tap is turned on only two-thirds of the way. Use reflectors behind gas brackets. When the gas oven is heated put the baking sheet out of the oven over the gas ring, and one burner will then keep several saucepans boiling.

141. **To Mend China.**—White lead is excellent for repairing china. Have the fractured edges clean and dry, then smear with a little of the white lead. Press the parts well together, holding them in place with rubber bands or string. Allow at least a month to harden. After this the repair will be complete, and the article can be washed in hot water without any risk.

142. **To Keep Milk Fresh.**—To prevent milk from turning during hot weather, make up sufficient water-glass as required to double strength—that is, only add half the water stated in the directions on the tins. Place the mixture in a pail or bowl and stand your milk jug in it. You must not let the mixture reach the top of the jug. This mixture will last through the summer.

143. **To Remove Various Stains.**—Blood stains: apply cold water at once. Coffee stains: pour boiling water over. Cocoa stains: wash in cold, and then pour on boiling water. Fruit stains: pour on boiling water. Grass stains: damp with cold water and apply cream of tartar. Ink stains: soak in milk or lemon-juice, and a little salt. Red Ink stains: Apply ammonia and water, then wash in milk.

144. **To Save Coal.**—Half a teaspoonful of saltpetre mixed in half a cupful of warm water and poured on a scuttle of coal will induce a brighter fire and make the coal last longer. Also, a good handful of ordinary washing soda dissolved in half a bucket of warm water, thrown over a hundredweight of coal and allowed to dry, will make the coal last half as long again. Mix some coal dust and clay together with water, finally covering the mixture with coal dust. Make it up into round balls to fit your stove ; they will keep your fire in, give out a good heat, and will effect a saving in your coal bill.

145. **Furniture Revivers.**—Wash the furniture well with vinegar and water and dry it thoroughly. Cut one and a half ounces of soap into tiny pieces and place into a jam jar, add half an ounce each of shredded beeswax and white wax, and a teacupful of boiling water ; stand the jar in boiling water until the ingredients have dissolved. When quite cold, add a dessertspoonful of methylated spirits and a cupful of turpentine (these two ingredients being inflammable they must be kept away from the fire or gas). Apply polish to the furniture with a soft rag, rub it in, and polish with tissue paper. Though cheap to prepare it will be found excellent to use.

146. **How to Treat Furs.**—Shake the fur well, brush and comb it, then lay it flat on sheets of newspaper. Sprinkle some powdered bitter apple (obtainable from the

chemist) over the fur. If camphor is used several cubes must be placed in the folds of the fur, which should then be wrapped up and secured with string. Furs should be hung up in dark blue or purple bags, not laid in drawers.

147. **How to Store Furs.**—Lay a large sheet of newspaper on the table, and place the well-shaken furs on top. Then get half a pound of carbon balls, and crush to a fine powder. Put carbon powder in a tin and make some holes in the lid. Then shake well into the furs, using all the carbon. Place another sheet of newspaper on top ; make a hem all the way round, sew the furs into the paper, and put away until wanted.

148. **Darning Hints.**—For darning wool vests, pants, combinations, etc., buy fine wool in skeins, which should be tied in one or two places to prevent entangling. Pour boiling water over them, and let them remain for a few minutes ; take out, allow to drip and dry in the open-air. Wool can be taken off cards, tied in skeins, and then shrunk. This treatment will entirely prevent the hardness and puckering so often seen on men's vests in the under arm. Darn closely with a *fine* needle and never use double wool. It is much easier and quicker to darn thin places than to darn a big hole, and the work has a neater appearance. Darn loosely, and leave a small loop in the wool at each end.

149. **A Soap to Keep the Hands Soft.**—Collect any small oddments of preservene soap, add half their weight in oatmeal, put the soap into a pan with a little water to dissolve, stir over a very low gas jet, and when melted, add the oatmeal ; mix well and turn out on a piece of wood to cool. Divide it into small cakes with a sharp knife, and leave it there several days to set before using.

150. **To Clean Tiles.**—If glazed tiles are spotted, they should be cleaned by rubbing them over with a cut lemon.

Leave them for a quarter of an hour or more, and polish with a soft dry cloth.

151. **To Clean Varnished Paint Work.**—Tea leaves are invaluable as a means of cleaning varnished paint. Save all the tea leaves for a day or two, put them in a bucket and soak them in water ; soak half an hour, then strain, and use the tea instead of soap and water.

152. **To Clean the Bars of a Stove.**—To remedy the burnt and untidy appearance of the bars of a grate, rub them with a piece of lemon before applying the blacklead, they will then polish very easily.

153. **Grease Spots on Old Oak.**—Warm a little ordinary beer, and rub well over the stains ; polish with a soft duster.

154. **To Clean Saucepans.**—Fill saucepan with hot water, shred in some preservene soap, boil until dissolved, let it remain over night and the saucepan will be snow-white inside. After scraping the dirt from the soap-jelly, the latter can be used for any household work. This treatment is equally good for aluminium ware, and materially lengthens the life of pots and pans.

155. **To Press Men's Trousers.**—Use a clean ironing sheet. Brush the trousers well and spread them out flat on the sheet. Do each leg separately, wring a clean cloth out in cold water and spread over one leg, see that there are no creases. Press well with a hot iron until there is no water left in the cloth. Do not rub the iron up and down or you will stretch the cloth, but press and lift the iron until you have gone all over the trouser leg. When the other leg has been treated in the same manner, shake out the steam and lay both legs on the sheet and press under a dry cloth. When perfectly dry, brush again.

156. **Shampoo for the Hair.**—Take a small piece of preservene soap, cut it into thin flakes or chips ; put the flakes into a jug filled with boiling water, stir with an old spoon until the soap has melted. You will then have a lovely creamy lather.

157. **A Bilious Headache.**—A teaspoonful of lemon-juice will often relieve a headache.

158. **To Prevent Chilblains.**—Rub the hands and feet with damp salt.

159. **To Keep a Doorstep White** in wet weather. Use plaster of Paris instead of whitening.

160. **A Burnt Preserving Pan Hint.**—Should you burn the bottom of your enamel preserving pan, get a packet of chloride of lime, put in the pan, with about a quart of water, and let it soak for two or three days. Give the pan a good rubbing and the burnt marks will have disappeared.

161. **To Remove the Odour of Fish from Silver-ware.**—Add a spoonful of mustard in the washing-up water.

162. **To Remove Sea-Water Stains from Shoes.**—Dissolve a small piece of washing soda in an egg cup of hot milk.    While the mixture is warm apply it with a cloth to the stains, and rub in well. When dry, clean the shoes with ordinary polish.

163. **White Furniture.**—Dissolve a little whitening in warm water, rub this on with a cloth and it will restore its whiteness and help to preserve the enamel.

164. **To Prevent Having Chapped Hands.**—Keep a large jar of oatmeal beside the sink, and the bathroom basin. After drying the hands, plunge them into the oatmeal and rub it into the skin.

165. **To Keep Flies Off Windows and Mirrors.**—Sprinkle a little vinegar on the washing leather when cleaning them. This is especially useful during the summer months.

166. **To Save White-washing Ceiling when it has Become Soiled over Gas.**—Make a thick starch, and apply to the soiled part of the ceiling. When dry, brush off and there will be no traces of smoke.

167. **A Glove Hint.**—To prolong the wear of gloves place a small piece of cotton wool in the tips of each finger and thumb to prevent the nails rubbing through.

168. **Pips for flavouring.**—Pound your apple and orange pips and add them to a tart for flavouring.

169. **Hint for Drying Wet Boots.**—Wet boots should never be put before the fire. To dry properly fill them with oats. These absorb the moisture and swell, so that the boots are filled out as though they have wooden trees in them. The same oats can be used again after drying.

170. **Slate and Pencil for Kitchen.**—Have a slate and pencil hanging on the kitchen wall, and when household articles become used up or nearly so, just jot it down on your slate. This will save endless worry when the weekly order has to be made out for the grocer, baker, butcher, etc.

171. **When Buying New Socks or Stockings.**—Buy a card of wool or silk of the same shade. Take running stitches across each heel and this doubles the life of every pair.

172. **Washing-up.**—Much trouble can be saved when washing up by taking a piece of paper and wiping all greasy plates first. This is very useful in the country, where one has no hot water tap.

173. **To mend loose knife blades** make a mixture of four parts resin, one part beeswax, and one part plaster of paris. Fill the hole in the middle with this. Then heat the tang and press it into the handle. Leave to set.

174. **To prevent Jam going mouldy on top** soak the parchment rounds in milk.

175. **To Prevent Milk from Burning.**—Milk will not burn if you sprinkle a little sugar over the bottom of the pan before you put the milk in.

176. **To Stop Cabbage from Boiling Over.**—Put a piece of butter or dripping the size of a walnut into the water as soon as it comes to the boil.

177. **When the Rollers of a Wringer Become Worn,** a good way to renovate them is to get some strips of calico, and sew neatly round the rollers. This will make the worn part perfectly smooth and prevent the wood from damaging the clothes.

178. **Detached Umbrella Handle.**—If the handle of an umbrella becomes detached do not put it aside, but mend it. Fill up the hole with brimstone, heat the screw red-hot and press it into the cavity. When cold it will be quite firm and hard.

179. **Make Your Own Soap Flakes.**—Shred a bar of preservene soap with a suet grater. Keep in a box so that a handful of the flakes can be taken at any moment.

180. **To Prevent Soiling the Woodwork when Cleaning Brass Knocker.**—Make a shield of stiff cardboard by cutting a hole same size and shape as the brass surround. This will serve for years if not lost.

181. **Sheet Tin for Stove or Table.** Sheet tin is a great help in a kitchen. Have one piece for top of stove. Several saucepans can boil at one time on it with the use

of only one gas burner ; also have a piece for the table. Stand stewpots, saucepans on it while cooking. This saves time in scrubbing table. A wipe over with newspaper will clean the tin.

182. **Small Table on Castors.**—A small light table on castors is a great help in a large kitchen. It can be wheeled to the sink when washing-up or preparing vegetables ; also to the cupboard or plate rack with clean pots, or to fire and oven with food ready for cooking.

183. **To Clean Tables, Boards, etc.**—Scrub tables, boards, with a mixture of melted preservene soap and sand. This makes then perfectly clean. It is good also for stained hands.

184. **Use Labour-saving Dusters.**—Soak some soft muslin cloth in paraffin ; dry out doors. Used for dusting, furniture will seldom require polishing. Soak soft lining cloth in hartshorn. Use for rubbing up silver, will not require weekly cleaning then.

185. **A Sink Hint.**—A lump of soda laid upon the sink-pipe, down which waste water passes, will prevent the clogging of the pipe with grease.

186. **Grease Spilt on Table.**—If the cook has the misfortune to spill grease on the kitchen table, she may save herself a great deal of trouble by sprinkling the stain at once with coarse salt ; this prevents the grease from sinking into the wood ; or, if spilled on the floor, dash cold water over it, so as to harden it quickly, and prevent its sinking into the boards.

187. **To prevent Candied Jam** soak the parchment rounds in vinegar instead of water. Another method is to cover your jam while it is hot.

188. **A Rickety Looking-Glass.**—Sometimes a looking-glass loses "the grip" and will not stay in position, the screw behind being useless. Tie a coloured ribbon round the middle of a cork and hang it at the side. Place it in proper position between the glass and stand, and your trouble is at an end.

189. **Prevent Cakes from Burning.**—Place a shallow tin filled with salt at the bottom of the oven when baking cakes.

190. **Oilcloth Apron.**—Always wear a large apron of white oilcloth when washing. This prevents wetting and soiling dress.

191. **A Handy Adhesive.**—Take a small piece of cold potato which has been boiled, and rub it up and down a piece of paper with your fingers for two or three minutes. It will become the right consistency and stick as well as the strongest glue.

192. **Keeping Cupboard Dry.**—To absorb damp in a cupboard, fill a box with lime, and place upon a shelf. This will result in the air in the cupboard being kept both dry and sweet.

193. **To Retain the Gloss on Silk Blouses.**—Before washing add a small quantity of methylated spirits to the water; then wash in a lather of preservene soap and rinse well. This will tend to preserve the glossy character of the silk.

194. **Burning Chimney.**—To put out a burning chimney throw about a pound of ordinary washing soda, well-damped, on the fire. The fumes extinguish the flames.

195. **To Loosen Glass Stoppers, Rusty Screws, etc.**—Pour on a little vinegar, then turn sharply. The result is surprising.

196. **When Storing Fine Linen.**—Linen that is not in constant use should be wrapped in something blue to preserve the colour and prevent its becoming yellow. Blue paper will do, or part of an old sheet that has been previously dipped in deep blue water.

197. **When Baking Fish.**—Line the baking tin or dish with a piece of strong, white paper, greased with a little oil or butter. Lay the fish with any accessories on the top of this, and you will find that it is easily removed when cooked. Also, when the paper is slipped out, the tin or dish is left comparatively clean and can be easily washed without the usual scraping.

198. **When Fires Won't Burn.**—This may be due to several causes—damp wood, insufficient paper, a damp chimney, or careless laying. If the chimney is damp, roll up a piece of newspaper loosely, light it, and allow it to burn as it goes up the chimney, just as the fire is lighted. If it is a kitchen range, open the flue door at the back of the stove and put the lighted paper up; this warms the chimney slightly and creates an upward draught. If the wood is damp and no dry wood is available, roll up some balls of newspaper rather tightly, and carefully arranged small pieces of coal on these. In quite a short time there will be a good fire. An old metal tray or sheet of metal held across the front of an open fire produces a good draught.

199. **A Curtain Hint.**—If the casement rod is difficult to pass through a curtain hem, as is sometimes the case with newly washed thin ones, put a large thimble on the end of the rod and it will slip along easily.

200. **To Clear a Room of Flies.**—Tie a wine-glass, broken at the base of the stem to a light pole, long enough to reach the ceiling. After sunset or in the early morning

when the flies are asleep on the ceiling, hold the glass half full of methylated spirits under the flies. The fumes will cause the flies to fall into the spirit, which kills them instantly. The spirit can be poured off into a bottle and used over and over again. A room can be cleared of flies in this way in two minutes.

201. **To Remove Paint from Window Panes.**—Take a thick piece of pencil eraser and rub the marks lightly. They will quickly disappear without leaving any scratch. Varnish stains can be removed in the same way.

202. **To Wash Velveteen.**—Make a good lather of preservene, place the velveteen in it, and move it about well. Take out but do not wring it; put it in clean water and move well about. Take it out and put it to dry without wringing. When nearly dry shake well, and when dry it is equal to new.

203. **When Using Valuable Vases for Table Decorations** fill them with sand, for this makes them stand firmly and renders them less likely to be knocked over and broken.

204. **Uses of Salt.**—Salt thrown on soot which has fallen on the carpet will prevent stains. Salt put on ink which has been freshly spilt on a carpet will help in removing the spot. Salt puts out a fire in the chimney. Salt and vinegar will remove stains from discoloured teacups. Salt as a gargle will remove soreness in throat. Salt used in sweeping carpets will keep out moths.

205. **A Cheese Hint.**—If a piece of cheese is carefully wrapped in a cloth wrung out in vinegar it will neither dry nor gather mould.

206. **To make a Stale Loaf like new** dip it quickly in and out of cold water and bake it in a moderate oven until crisp.

207. **A Tablecloth Hint.**—To hide an isolated fruit stain on a fresh tablecloth, cover with a piece of white stamp paper. This will not show and will come off in the wash.

208. **A Jam Hint.**—Lemon juice added to jam when boiling will help the jam to jelly, and also improve the flavour.

209. **When Cooking Vegetables.**—All vegetables grown above ground should be boiled with the lid off the saucepan while those grown under should have the lid kept on.

210. **Linen with Coloured Borders.**—Housewives will find that household linen with red borders will run, thus staining other linen with which they may be washed. If, when new, before being washed, they are steeped in a gallon of water containing a good handful of common salt for twenty-four hours, this trouble is overcome, and they may be washed afterwards with any linen without fear of the red design staining other things. This method makes the colour fast.

211. **Coal Dust for Fire Grate.**—If you have a quantity of small coal dust, put it in a strong paper bag, or fold it in a newspaper before you place it on the fire. Do not disturb it, and you will find that it will cake together instead of slipping through the bars. This is a good way of keeping in the fire when not needed for cooking.

212. **An Easy Way to Peel Apples.**—Pour scalding water over the apples, and then the skin may easily be slipped off and much labour and waste saved.

213. **To Preserve Life of Stair Carpet.**—When buying allow at least one yard more than necessary (this more than pays the extra cost in the wear). Frequently take up, beat, wash over with preservene soap, when any stain will disappear and colours brighten. Alter tread and place of

stair rods by moving the carpet up or down a little. Never put down again in exactly the same position as before (the yard extra allows for this easily).

214. **To Re-dip Tape and Cord of Venetian Blind.**—Mix a little yellow ochre with water. If wanted a dark brown shade put in a little vinegar. Either put tapes and cord into the mixture ; or, of not taken down, rub well into them with piece of flannel.

215. **To Preserve Linoleum and Oilcloth.**—Wash well with preservene soap. When thoroughly dry give coat of quick drying varnish (spirit varnish) and it will only be necessary to rub up with a duster for weeks, then polish.

216. **Tight-fitting Drawers.**—Rub preservene soap along the upper edges of the drawer. They will then run smoothly and the smell will act as a preventative against moths.

217. **To Prevent a Wire Mattress Getting Rusty.**—If a wire mattress gets rusty, give it a coat of aluminium paint, and it will never give any further trouble.

218. **Weights and Measures.**—Many a housewife is puzzled by directions which give weights of liquids. How is water to be weighed ? Don't weigh it—measure it, and here is your measure :—1 tablespoonful liquid weighs $\frac{1}{2}$ oz., 1 dessertspoonful liquid weighs $\frac{1}{4}$ oz., 1 teaspoonful liquid weighs $\frac{1}{8}$ oz.

219. **When Wringing and Mangling Tablecloths,** Towels and Sheets, do not fold then always in the same way week after week, but fold them alternately, one week by the hem and the next week by the selvedge. This will make them wear twice as long.

220. **To Restore Colour.** Alum-water will restore any faded colour if put into the rinsing water after the clothes are washed.

221. **A Quick Polish to your Shoes or Boots.**—Dip your blacking brush in a little lemon or orange juice after it has been in the blacking or cream.

222. **To cure Hiccoughs.**—Drink half a teaspoonful of vinegar and hold the hands above the head for a minute or two.

223. **Hot-water Bottles.**—Do not discard when cracked, but fill with sand and heat in slow oven.

224. **To Preserve Apples.**—To preserve apples during the winter months they should first be rubbed with glycerine, then placed on shelves. Leave a small space between each, to prevent rotting.

225. **To Clean a White Felt Hat.**—Rub it all over with powdered magnesia leave it on for a day ; shake well and remove all powder with a stiff brush.

226. **To Keep Game Fresh.**—Newly ground coffee sprinkled over game will keep it fresh.

227. **Damp the edges of the pastry for your tart** with milk instead of water, then the fruit will not boil over so easily.

228. **Lemons** will keep fresh for a considerable time if covered with water, which is changed daily.

229. **If Meat is Tough** put a tablespoonful of vinegar over it. The meat will be very tender when done.

230. **Kitchen tables** which have got discoloured can be brought back to their snow-white pitch if well scrubbed with lime water. Buy 3d. of lime, to which add water and let stand half a day. Strain off and use as ordinary water, but be careful not to get much on the hands as it burns.

231. **How to Wash Blankets.**—Slice half-pound of preservene soap into two quarts of water. Set the pan on the stove and stir till the soap is dissolved. Put solution into a tub of cold water with four tablespoonsful of borax. Then put in blankets and let them soak all night. Next day wash in same water, rinse twice in clean cold water. Do not wring. Hang on line to dry. This quantity of soap and borax will wash four blankets.

232. **To Clean Knives.**—Take a potato and cut a small piece off one end. Dip the cut end of the potato into some knife powder. Hold the knife firmly on a flat surface (the end of the sink is a good place as it can be so easily wiped clean afterwards). Rub the powdered end of the potato on the blade of the knife, then turn it over and repeat the process.

233. **Mildew** can be removed by soaking the affected garment in buttermilk.

234. **Cleaning Men's Suits.**—First brush the garments well, turn pockets inside-out, and brush and shake. Lay them flat on a kitchen table and sponge carefully with preservene soap in the following manner. Cut up half cake of soap finely into about a pint of cold water and stir over gentle heat till dissolved. Turn this into a basin and allow to get cold. Dip a small stiff nailbrush into this jelly and rub gently the dirty spots ; take a clean sponge and dip in cold water and sponge till soap disappears. Press with hot iron and the suit is almost equal to new.

235. **The Best Way to Wash Lace.**—Put the lace into a wide-necked bottle (a milk bottle is splendid if you have a cork which will fit tightly into the top). Then pour in enough warm lather, made from preservene soap, to fill the bottle three-quarters full. Now cork it up well and shake the bottle backwards and forwards, holding the palm of the hand over the cork. The movement should not be too

vigorous. If the lace is very dirty it may need a second bath of lather. Drain off the soapy water, then three-quarters fill the bottle with fresh warm water. Rinse the lace in this, drain well and give in final rinse in clear cold water. Last of all, shake the lace out on a soft clean towel slightly warmed and wrap it up.

236. **After Washing Soft Net or Muslin Curtains** hang them up at the widow in a wet state ; then run a heavy stick or pole through the hem at the bottom. When dry remove the pole and the curtains will delight your eye.

237. **To Remove Perspiration Stains.**—If a garment has become badly stained with perspiration do not attempt to wash it until the stain has been treated. Soak the part for about a quarter of an hour in clear, cold water, then rub with a cut juicy lemon. Let the lemon juice soak well in, but not for more than a minute or two. Rinse thoroughly in cold water. Wash as usual.

238. **A Shiny Coat Collar** can be cleaned by sponging it with a cloth moistened with ammonia or vinegar.

239. **Hot Vinegar.**—Paint can be removed from windows with hot vinegar. Paint brushes which have become hard will soften if immersed in hot vinegar.

240. **Wall-paper Patching.**—If a wallpaper has to be patched to hide a stain or injury, tear the paper irregularly. The edges will be less noticeable than those of a rectangular piece. This is a hint worth noting and putting into practice.

241. **To Keep a Saucepan Lid Raised While Cooking.**— A useful article for keeping the lid of a saucepan raised as one often wants to do while cooking can be made out of an ordinary clothes peg, reducing the prongs to one inch in length. Fix the peg over the edge of the pan as if it were a clothes line.

242. **Hole in Bath or Bucket.**—Clean the article round hole, take a small piece of putty and spread over hole, making neat and tidy. Leave to dry a few days, but not by gas or fire, or the putty will crack. In a few days the putty will be quite dry and hard. Things repaired in this way will last years.

243. **To Prevent Burning Christmas Cakes, etc.**—If when baking a Christmas or Birthday cake, ground rice cake, jam roly-poly, or anything of that description, an enamelled pie-dish full of water is placed in the lower part of the oven, any of the above can be baked thoroughly without any risk of burning.

244. **Hint for Parsley Sauce.**—When making parsley sauce, time can be saved and the sauce greatly improved by this method : Instead of chopping parsley, take it from the stalk and drop into boiling water, to which a pinch of salt and a tiny piece of soda have been added. Boil a few minutes. Then stir into melted butter. The parsley dissolves into tiny shreds and the colour and flavour is very much better than when made in the old style.

245. **Mending Children's Boots.**—When the toecaps of children's boots or shoes split, which often occurs while uppers and soles are still in good condition, thus making them look shabby, take a piece of an old kid glove (either black or brown) the size required and smear the back with any liquid cement. Then, with the aid of a penknife or tips of small scissors, slip underneath the broken part, smear edges of upper, and press well on to the patch. Leave to dry, polish afterwards, when it will hardly be noticed.

246. **Re-papering Over Damp Patches.**—Before re-papering a room or cupboard, give the bare walls where dampness has appeared, three coats of waterglass, such as is used for preserving eggs. Be sure each coating is dry

before another is applied. Dampness will never penetrate after this treatment, which is a boon and blessing to people who live in damp houses.

247. **To Wash Lace Curtains.**—Wash the curtains thoroughly with preservene soap. When clean, starch and then squeeze as much water as possible from them. Do not hang out of doors to dry, but put up at the windows while still wet. Pull into shape and arrange as desired. This saves the trouble of hanging out and ironing. When dry the curtains look quite as well as if they had been ironed.

248. **To Keep Brasses Clean.**—After the brasses have been cleaned in the usual way, a little olive oil rubbed over taps, brass plates, etc., will keep then bright for some time, so that it is not necessary to clean them every day.

249. **Silk Garments** will iron up like new if a little methylated spirit is added to the rinsing water.

250. **To Clean Old Brass.**—Save labour in cleaning old brass by pouring strong ammonia on it. Use a scrubbing brush and rinse in clear water.

251. **A Kitchen Fender** often rusts from kettle splashes, etc. A great deal of cleaning may be saved by giving the fender two coats of lacquer.

252. **To Remove Mildew.**—A little while ago I had a sheet covered all over with Mildew. I tried all sorts of remedies, but of no avail. Then I tried preservene. I boiled the sheet for half an hour in a good lather of preservene. Rinsed in clear water and put it on the grass to dry. When done the mildew had completely disappeared.

253. **Drying Clothes Without Pegs.**—The method of drying clothes on a line without the use of pegs is used by the natives of India and Japan. Two thinnish ropes are taken and twisted together before fixing to the clothes'

posts. The corners of the article to be dried are pushed in between the twists of the ropes by means of first fingers and thumb, and is very rapidly done by the experienced " washerman." It is found that the friction between the two ropes is sufficient to hold any reasonably light article against a strong wind, and no damage whatever is done to the article. In removing clothes from the line it is only necessary to walk from one end of the line to the other, gathering the clothes over the shoulder in transit, as removal from the line by hand is quite unnecessary.

254. **To Open a Tin Easily.**—Does your boot-polish or floor-polish tin stick tight ? If this is the case, a good plan, when you have first got the lid off, is to place a small tab of tape between the lid and the bottom of the tin. You will then be able to lift the lid off quite easily by pulling up the tab.

255. **A Household Hint.**—**Clothes Baskets.**—Have you noticed the bottom of your clothes basket wears first, due to the weight and friction caused by dragging the basket along the floor or garden, when hanging out the clothes. If the basket is kept clear of the ground it will last much longer. To do this, either place battens across the bottom, or insert four stout pegs in the plaiting of the basket.

256. **To Save Gas.**—Have all saucepans and kettles for use on the gas stove made of tin, with copper bottoms slightly concave. This draws the gas up under the vessel and saves a great deal of gas. A three-pint kettle made thus boils three minutes quicker than one made in the ordinary way, which means a great deal saved in gas in the year. Saucepans and kettles made in this way cost no more than those made with flat bottoms.

257. **Washing Lace Curtains.**—To do up lace curtains without stretchers, wash in preservene soap—no rubbing is required. Starch without wringing, and hang lengthwise

on the line. Place opposite scallops together, then pull the curtain straight. The starch will stick the opposite sides together. Use no pins ; the curtains will be straight and even ; no ironing required ; just the pressing of the scallops.

258. **What Starch Can Do.**—Powdered starch is an excellent silver polish, and it removes stains from wallpaper when nothing else will, while if when washing windows a lump of starch is added to the water, the dirt will be removed more easily. Boiled starch rubbed over newly washed linoleum will put a skin on it if allowed to dry for an hour or two, and it can then be polished with beeswax and turpentine.

259. **Scorch Marks in Linen** may be removed by rubbing with a freshly cut onion and afterwards soaking in cold water.

260. **To Remove Inkstains.**—It is very annoying when children return from school with their light clothes splashed with ink. If article is white, half fill a bucket with cold water, shred in a little preservene soap, place article in water. Put the bucket on gas ring and boil for fifteen minutes—not a sign of ink remains. (If coloured light clothes, soak in luke-warm milk, and wash afterwards. Once a bottle of red ink was spilt over a pink frock, but it came out with milk, leaving no stain.)

261. **Cooking a Joint.**—For years I have always cooked my joints between two meat or oven tins of the same size, use rather a lot of dripping. Take off top tin last quarter of hour for meat to crisp. Even the toughest joints come out beautifully tender, as they are roasted and steamed at same time.

262. **Meat Cooked in Own Juice.**—This is delicious and highly nutritious. When stewing beef, chops, etc., try

this way. Either use a stew jar with lid, or jam jar. Cut up (if beef), place in jar with dessertspoonful water ; cut up onions finely (if any), put on lid, or place grease paper over, place in boiling water half way up and steam for three hours ; season with salt and pepper and serve. It fairly melts in mouth.

263. **A Five-Minute Pudding.**—Perhaps someone drops in just after dinner is finished. You can heat up the meat, but most likely the pudding is all eaten. Beat up an egg, fill up cup with cold milk, sweeten and stir egg in. Place cup in small saucepan, with boiling water nearly half way up. Put saucepan lid on. Place over small light on gas ring ; in five minutes you have a well set custard.

264. **Handy China Cement.**—This preparation is colourless and wonderfully strong. Dissolve $\frac{1}{2}$ oz. gum arabic in a wineglass of boiling water ; add enough plaster of Paris to make a thick paste. Apply to the broken parts with a brush, press together with a firm and steady pressure, and when dry the join will be invisible.

265. **To Prevent Grease Splashing When Frying.**—When frying bacon, fish, etc., put a bit of bread in the pan and fry it at the same time. It will prevent the grease from splashing out on to the stove and so save a lot of unnecessary labour in cleaning and polishing the stove afterwards.

266. **Use a Drainer.**—Washing-up becomes a pleasure if one possess a wooden drainer for plates and cups. These can be purchased cheaply at any London store.

267. **Ink Stains on Books** may be removed by a solution of oxalic acid in water.

268. **To Remove Grass Stains.** Rub on plenty of treacle and afterwards wash the garment in tepid water.

269. **To Shine Damp Boots.**—Boots and shoes however damp will polish in a few minutes if a drop or two of paraffin oil be added to the blacking. Furthermore, it prevents the leather from cracking.

270. **A Novel Way of Heating an Invalid's Room.**— Put a block of salt in the grate ; pour on as much paraffin as it will absorb ; set a match to it, and a steady clear glow is the result. The salt must be moistened every night. It will gradually wear away and want replacing in about three weeks. You have a warm bedroom with very little trouble and no dust or dirt.

271. **To Prevent Steam from Settling on your Eyeglasses** whilst cooking or entering a hot room, slightly rub a little preservene soap on the glass with the tip of your finger then polish with a clean soft rag.

272. **To Prevent a Candle Dripping.**—If a little common salt is put round the top of the candle before lighting it will not drip at all.

273. **For Cleaning a Velour Hat.**—Do not wash it, but brush on a thick lather of preservene soap, then dry with a clean cloth ; repeat if necessary. Let the hat dry thoroughly then brush with a wire brush. It will look like new.

274. **Handkerchiefs** need no ironing if they are spread out quite flat on a hot cylinder or mirror when they are still wet after washing. They will be dry in a few minutes and will have every appearance of having been exceptionally well ironed. Any small articles such as muslin or soft linen collars, etc., may be treated successfully in the same way. Failing a hot cylinder, a mirror will do almost equally well.

275. **Cleaning—Without Cleaner's Bills.**—To clean men's overcoats, spats, etc.; men's tweed, cloth, felt and velour hats; Bedford cord upholstery in motor cars; leather cloth upholstery in motor cars and suites; woollen tapestry upholstery on Chesterfield suites: Place small articles on firm flat surface after first brushing out all loose dust. Wring out clean cloth in hot water and rub well with preservene soap. Evenly rub article, paying particular attention to dirty spots or streaks, and frequently rinse out cloth, applying soap freely, but take care not to wet the article too much. When clean, rinse fresh clean cloth in clear cold water to which salt has been added, and rub all over, rinsing cloth frequently. Place in warm, airy place to dry, preferably out of doors on a dry, windy day. Hats should be placed on flat surface in the desired correct shape and finished by being brushed, when dry, with clean soft brush, to raise pile. Leather should be rubbed with furniture polish when dry, and polished with soft, warm duster. NOTE.—Carpets may be treated in the above manner and will look like new.

276. **To thread a needle quickly.**—Many precious moments are often lost in threading a darning needle. Next time try the following way and see how it helps. Pass the two ends of a short cotton thread through the needle, then slip the wool through the loop of the thread, holding the two ends of the thread. Pull the thread through the eye of the needle and your wool is through with it.

277. **To Save the Trouble of Damping Clothes,** e.g., handkerchiefs, etc., leave one fairly wet, and roll the others round. The moisture passes through and thus damps all the handkerchiefs. Saving about ten minutes with this small idea.

**278. To Mend a Cotton Blind.**—Many people do not know that the easiest and quickest way to mend a cotton blind is to take a piece of the same material, soak it in boiling starch, wring dry, and place over tear, then iron with hot iron. This is a much quicker, better and easier way of mending such torn articles than using needle and cotton.

**279. To Frost Windows.**—Make a strong mixture of vinegar and Epsom Salts and paint with cloth.

**280. To Remove Onion Smell.**—After peeling onions rub hands well with celery to remove odour.

**281. How To Keep a Bath Clean.**—If a bath already bears signs of a " tide-mark," the first thing to do is to clean it with a drop of paraffin and hot water. The cause of the water-mark remaining is not from actual use of the bath, but is due to dust that settles during the day, so to keep the bath nice and clean, sponge it out, right to the top immediately before using, and again when finished with a sponge kept for the purpose. Clean right to the top, otherwise the mark will stay where the sponging ends.

**282. Soapsuds for the Garden.**—After the washing is done, water rose trees, shrubs and fruit trees with the cold soapsuds, instead of throwing them away.

**283. When making Cake Icing** pour the egg whites over the icing sugar and leave standing as long as possible. This method saves much rolling and pounding out of lumps.

**284. Jam Pot Covers.**—Butter paper or plain white notepaper dipped into milk, and pressed down on to the jars make excellent jam pot covers, as they dry like parchment and are therefore stronger than ordinary jam pot covers.

285. **Nail Holes in Woodwork.**—Mix some sawdust with a little glue to the consistency of thick paste. Press the compound into the holes, and it will become as hard as the wood.

286. **To Set a Jelly.**—When a jelly will not set, add the juice of a lemon, and the difficulty will be overcome.

287. **An Excellent Way to Empty the Copper.**—Fill a short length of hosepipe with water, and, holding one end, place at the bottom of the full copper. Then let the other end drop over the top of the copper into the sink, and the water will continue to run out until the copper is empty. This is much quicker than dipping it up with a dipper, and saves much time and labour.

288. **A Baking Hint.**—If salt is placed in the tin it prevents burning contents, and a dish of water placed in oven prevents cakes scorching.

289. **To Preserve Beetroot.**—Put half teaspoonful of mustard in muslin bag. Place in jar with the cooked beetroot, and it will prevent it turning mouldy.

290. **Fish Saucepans.** To clean, fill with cold water and little vinegar, and let it boil. All smell and taste will disappear.

291. **Glass Dishes.**—Place these on wet cloth when putting hot fruit in them so as to prevent cracking.

292. **To Clean Kettles.**—Fill them with potato parings and boil fast till quite clean.

293. **Omelettes (to Prevent Burning).**—Warm the pan and rub with soft paper and salt, then grease another paper with lard, and rub dry and the omelette will not burn.

294. **To remove Ironmould Stains.**—Mix equal quantities of liquid ammonia with iodine and apply to the stains. Afterwards rinse the article in plenty of water, then wash well in soap and water. Give a thorough final rinsing in clear water.

295. **To Clean Painted Woodwork.**—When cleaning painted woodwork add a little paraffin to the water. This not only removes the dirt, but leaves no smears and also preserves the paint and varnish.

296. **To Clean Small Articles of Lacquered Brass.**—Boil a few minutes in vinegar and rinse in plenty of cold water. Hot vinegar may be applied to large articles of brassware with good results.

297. **When Washing Blankets** a jelly should be made the day before by shredding a bar of preservene soap into a china vessel and covering it with boiling water. The following day place enough jelly to make a good lather in a bath of warm water. Two persons should well shake each blanket before it is immersed in water ; then work the blanket well in the suds, squeezing quite free from dirt. There should be two rinsing waters, the first warm and clear. A spoonful of glycerine may be added to each two gallons of second rinse water, but this is not necessary with preservene soap. Choose a fine windy day rather than a sunny day for washing blankets. Strong sunshine will harden the texture of woollen goods.

298. **To Drive Moths from Boxes and Drawers.**—Scatter cloves among the contents. This is more effective than naphtha.

299. **The Most Economical Way to Remove Stains from Saucepans,** both inside and out, is by rubbing with damp ashes. If ashes are unobtainable try rubbing with damp hearthstone.

300.  **When icing a cake** spread the icing over with a broad-bladed knife constantly dipped in hot water.  This method is easy and quick and the cake looks better when finished.

301.  **To Get Rid of Blackbeetles.**—Pour a hot solution of one pound of alum to three pints of boiling water into the cracks or seams where the insects appear.

302.  **Ironmould.**—Rhubarb juice is one of the best agents for removing ironmould.  Cut a stick of rhubarb into chunks and put them into a saucepan with a little water.  Boil briskly for a few minutes and then hold the stained linen in the hot solution for a few minutes.  Rinse with cold water and, if the ironmould does not yield, repeat the process until the yellow stain can be washed away.

303.  **To Remove Fruit Stains on Coloured Fabrics.**— Sponge fruit stains on coloured fabrics with ammonia and then with petrol.

304.  **Rolling-pin for Pastry.**—In hot weather a glass bottle used as a rolling pin for pastry helps to keep the pastry cool and light.  Choose as cool a place as possible for your rolling.

305.  **To Remove Flies.**—Flies will quickly disappear from a room if twenty drops of carbolic acid are evaporated from a hot shovel every day.

306.  **Coloured Clothes Fading.**—A teaspoonful of Epsom Salts added to each gallon of warm water will prevent the most delicate colours fading or running.  Vinegar will preserve or restore blue shades.  Always dry coloured clothes quickly and preferably in the shade.

307.  **Safety Pin Better Than Bodkin.**—Tape tied to a safety pin (closed) will go through the hem of a curtain more quickly and with less danger of tearing than if a bodkin is used.

308. **China and Glass.**—Add to tepid water a few drops of turpentine. Is splendid for washing china and glass. Use a chamois leather and have a deep bowl of water so that each article may be kept quite immersed. Dry and polish with a linen cloth.

309. **To Wash New Cotton Materials.**—Remove the dressing by soaking in cold water to which has been added a handful of Epsom Salts.

310. **To Remove Shine from Serge Garments.**—Boil ivy leaves and with the liquor sponge the shiny parts ; press while damp. The liquor may be used warm or cold.

311. **If Moths get into your Carpet, treat it** as follows : Put in a pail half a gallon of boiling water and a quarter of a pound of rock ammonia. Then take a large square of house-flannel and put it in the pail, leaving the ends hanging over the sides. Pick up the dry ends and wring the flannel. Place on the carpet and iron dry with a very hot iron. Go all over the carpet like this and no moths' eggs will come to life.

312. **To Use Candle Ends.**—Put a penny over the hole in candlestick and stand the candle end on it. It will burn to the last bit.

313. **Where Pantry and Kitchen Cupboards are Much Exposed** to dust, a good labour-saving device is to give the shelves a coat or two of white paint. One will do if the wood be smooth. Then finish off with a coat of white varnish paint or enamel. Instead of the weekly drudge of putting on clean papers, a cloth wrung out of warm water, with a rub of preservene soap will make them clean and fresh, which is so essential where food and stores are kept.

314. **Wheel Your Clothes to the Line.**—Do not throw away old pram. Take body off wheels and fix clothes basket in its place. This will be found very handy for

carrying clothes to drying ground. You can then wheel from place to place as you hang your clothes on the line.

315. **To Clear a Room of Flies.**—Put some eucalyptus oil on a cloth, open the door wide and wave the cloth vigorously working towards the door. The flies will rapidly disappear.

316. **An Emergency Nightlight** can be made from an ordinary candle. Allow the top to burn until it is quite even and then pile fine salt until only about a quarter of an inch of the wick projects. A candle treated in this way will give a steady light for many hours.

317. **After Peeling Onions.**—A little mustard well rubbed into the hands after peeling onions will remove the odour.

318. **To Prevent Tea Stains on Damask.**—A lump of sugar put in the tea-pot will prevent tea staining damask, however fine, over which it mày be spilt.

319. **To Keep Flies Away from Room.**—A fresh bunch of stinging nettles hung up in the window of a room will prevent the entrance of flies.

320. **A Potato Hint.**—Before frying cold potatoes, slice them and well dredge with flour. This not only causes the potatoes to brown more quickly but also improves their flavour.

321. **To Stone Raisins.**—Raisins will stone quite easily if warmed before stoning them.

322. **A Plum Pudding Hint.**—If a box pleat is put on the top of the cover of a plum or boiled pudding, it opens out as the pudding rises, and prevents the water from getting into the mixture.

323. **To Remove Egg Stains from Spoons and Forks.**— Take a little common salt between the thumb and finger and rub briskly.

324. **When making a Swiss Roll** or Jam Sandwich sprinkle flour over the greased tin. Your jam will spread more easily on the sandwich if it is heated.

325. **To Remove Rust from Steel knives.**—Rub with an onion and leave to stand. To polish tin also rub with an onion after dipping the tin into boiling soda water.

326. **A Useful Cement for Mending China, Glass, etc.,** can be obtained by melting alum in an old iron spoon over the fire.

327. **To Prevent New Earthenware from Cracking.**— Place the dishes in cold water and bring to the boil. Allow water to cool before removing dishes. New frying-pans are apt to warp. To prevent this cover the bottom with melted fat and boil for a few minutes.

328. **To Prevent Torn Edges on Paper Blinds.**—Paste some medium width tape down each edge.

329. **Before Lighting a Fire** hold a lighted screw of paper up the chimney. This creates a draught and prevents annoying puffs of smoke coming into the room.

330. **Roll Rubbish in Newspapers and Burn.**—It is well to burn all possible rubbish. Roll it tightly in several sheets of newspaper and place at the back of the fire. The paper soon becomes blackened and looks like coal.

331. **Always Keep a Lemon Handy.**—The juice will remove those horrid fruit and vegetable stains from the hands.

332. **Always Rinse the Milk Saucepan Out** with water before boiling the milk. This will help to prevent it burning.

333. **Do Not Use Pudding Cloths.**—Instead, cover with grease-proof paper, tie round with string, looping the ends across to form a handle. Turn up the edges of the paper in a neat roll. Allow the water to come only half-way up the basin.

334. **A Gas Stove Hint.**—Remove the iron cross-bar which passes across the gas ring on the gas stove. The heat taken up by the bar is thus saved. Note how much more quickly the kettle boils.

335. **Remove Smell of Smoking.**—At night place a bowl of water in a room where there has been smoking. The water will absorb the fumes and sweeten the room.

336. **To Keep Away Flies.**—Mignonette or a bunch of walnut leaves in a room discourages flies.

337. **To Clean Mechanic's Overalls** (a wrinkle).—I have successfully washed with preservene overalls which were absolutely refused by a laundry. They were thickly coated with dirt and grease. I followed the printed directions, but I pass on a wrinkle which helped me further still. Before putting the overalls into the boiler at the end of the wash, I wet them and soap well, all over, with another bar of preservene. During the boiling the dirt falls out, and in view of the filthy condition of the overalls the result is magical. An hour of back breaking labour saved.

338. **Eggs to Boil when Cracked.**—If you should happen to only have cracked eggs on hand and not the time to poach them, try the idea of wrapping each in a twist of tissue paper and boil in the usual way. You will not lose any of the contents.

339. **A Good Trouser Press Hint.**—Fold trousers and put legs (only) through wringer. This is equal to pressing and does not shine cloth. It takes four minutes in all.

340. **To Clean Strawberries.**—Soak in water to which a teaspoonful of vinegar has been added. It is surprising to see what insects there are hidden in the fruit. Wash in clear water and drain through sieve.

341. **Use for Old Stockings.**—The legs of old stockings can be stiched together by a sewing machine, and made into bloomers for little girls. They wear quite a long time, much better than serge as they stretch.

342. **Uses of Slacklime.**—Slacklime will remove rust from fireirons and steel fenders and grates. It also removes paint from woodwork, stains from marble washstands and fireplaces. It makes a good cement if mixed with the white of an egg for joining broken china.

343. **To Prevent Casseroles from Cracking.**—When new they should be well rubbed with a raw onion (this prevents vessel from sweating), fill with cold water, and gradually bring to boiling point ; then allow water to cool in vessel. Casseroles treated in this way will last for years.

344. **Jam Hint.**—Use a teaspoonful of glycerine to every pound of fruit. There will be less scum. Only ¾ lb. of sugar per pound of fruit is needed, and your jam will keep better.

345. **On Drying Silks.**—Never hang silk articles up to dry in the usual way, as they do not dry evenly and therefore when ironed it is found the hot iron required for the damp parts is scorching the dryer parts. Simply roll each article to be dried in a dry towel and leave them so overnight. When ironed the result is perfect, as the articles were an even dampness all over.

346. **To Iron Tussore Silks.**—It is often found that when these silks are ironed the result is a patchwork effect of various shades in tussore. The fault lies in the drying of the silk, which should always be *bone dry* before it is ironed. In this way a uniform shade of tussore is maintained throughout.

347. **Easy Varnishing for the Amateur.**—Heat the varnish in a warm oven before using. This diminishes the strong pull which the varnish has on the brush in its cold state, and makes the application of it much easier for the amateur.

348. **Renovating Shabby Wicker Chairs.**—First strip all cushions and covers from your chair, noting how they are sewn on, so that there will be no difficulty in replacing. Make a lather by shredding one-third of a bar of preservene into about two quarts of boiling water. Add cold water until required temperature is obtained. Wash cushions or covers in this lather, rinse, and if faded brighten by dipping into a dye-solution of a suitable shade. Carry your chair into the open and with a scrubbing brush and the remaining lather thoroughly cleanse the wicker, taking care to go into all the crevices ; wash off all the soap with clean warm water and leave in the air until quite dry. Now give it a coat of thin varnish, and when this is dry replace the clean cushions, and your old wicker chair will look like new.

349. **Dry Sand Will Extinguish Burning Oil.**—Where lamps are used, a bucketful of sand should always be kept in readiness in case of accident. Water is useless, for it has no effect whatever on flaming oil.

350. **When Buying Tinned Fruit,** press the bottom of the tin with the thumb. If it makes a noise like a machine oil-can when it is pressed, the tin is not airtight, and the contents are unfit for use.

351. **If a Teaspoonful of Methylated Spirit** is put into the rinsing water for white silk and coloured articles, it prevents the white from going yellow, and after ironing it imparts a gloss like new.

352. **To Wash Coloured Casement Curtains.**—Rub them well and leave overnight in cold water, with a pinch of salt. Next morning wash through a good lather of preservene soap and dry.

353. **The Hands.**—Equal parts of lemon juice, glycerine and Eau de Cologne makes a splendid lotion for the hands.

354. **To Remove Ironmould from Linen.**—Take the juice of a lemon and salt enough to cover the rust mark. Leave for a while, and it will all disappear.

355. **To Remove White Marks from Furniture** caused by water, take an equal amount of linseed oil and turpentine.

356. **Tea-stains** will suddenly disappear if soaped dry with preservene soap and dropped into the boiling copper to which preservene soap has been added.

357. **To Keep a Kitchen Clean.**—A shelf at back of gas stove, covered top and bottom with sheet zinc, which should be as wide as possible, up to 18 in. and 24 in. long or longer. This will keep the ceilings and walls clean and entirely free from the grease and dirt which comes from every gas stove oven.

358. **To Keep Door-step White.**—Painting door-step with flat white paint (which dries quickly). This used about twice monthly saves the labour of daily whitening and has a better appearance.

359. **How to Save Labour in Washing, Starching and Finishing Linens.**—Steep clothes in preservene cold water method—then rinse, blue, and hang out to dry. Take linens when perfectly dry and put through the following.

one teaspoonful starch, one teaspoonful dissolved borax, 1½ pints water (cold).   Then fold and put through wringer. They will now be easily ironed and will look as new.   This prolongs the life of linens as it does away with stretching and damping and is easy on the starch.

360.  **To Dust Rooms, etc., Quickly.**—Put a few drops of paraffin oil on the duster.  This makes dust cling to it and is easy to shake off.  Also is good for furniture.

361.  **Cakes—to prevent burning.**—To save trouble of having burnt cakes, put brick in oven, on which stand tins containing cake or bread.

362.  **Floor Mop—to make.**—Where there is no cedar mop for polishing floors, pad the head of an old soft broom.

363.  **Fish Drainer—to mend.**—A broken china fish drainer should be laced in place with fine string and tied.

364.  **To Clean Tea Kettles when Spouts are nearly Blocked.**—Fill with cold water and add half-pound of washing soda.  Boil for some hours.  Next day repeat. Then break off hard pieces with scissors.  Rinse and the spouts will pour out freely.

365.  **When Sweeping under Matting,** put down plenty of salt to keep dust from flying.

366.  **To Get Stains off Knives Quickly,** rub them with Brooks's soap.

367.  **To Save Feet Getting Over-tired** during ironing the clothes, stand on a cushion.

368.  **Where there is no Plate Rack,** drain plates and other table ware in wicker clothes basket.  This will also save going backwards and forwards, as many can be carried to right place at once.

369. **To Clean Glass Bottles.**—Nearly fill with warm water into which put enough shredded preservene soap to make good lather. Tear up small bits of tissue paper and put in. Well shake and rinse.

370. **Don't bang the oven door** when baking cakes; it stops them rising and makes them heavy.

371. **A Real Way to Get Rid of Beetles.**—Wash cupboards with some Jeyes' Fluid in water and wash floors with about tablespoonful of paraffin in water. This also for fleas, etc.

372. **To Peel Potatoes** use patent potato knife. This saves labour and keeps them a good shape.

373. **When Shirt Buttons Break.**—Shirt buttons are apt to be broken in the washing. A good way of preventing this is to make a small button-hole in place of the button and use a stud, or a link made of a large linen button and a small pearl one sewn together.

374. **To Wash a Satin Slip.**—To wash a satin slip successfully, soak for one and a half hours in soapy water, made by preservene soap, to which has been added $1\frac{1}{2}$ tablespoonsful of paraffin oil, $1\frac{1}{2}$ tabs. to three quarts of water. Then should come a gentle "swishing" about in soapy water without paraffin, and several rinsings in plain clear water to get it free of every bit of soap. Finally, it must be ironed almost dry on the wrong side, and the result will be a nice, fresh, new slip.

375. **To Make Glass-ware Brilliant.**—Use a tiny bit of blue in the water to wash it. Polish off with a soft cloth.

376. **To make your Bread-board white,** scrub the way of the grain with preservene soap, and leave in the open air to dry after rinsing.

377. **To Prevent a Steam-filled Bathroom.**—Fix a length of old rubber hose-piping on to the hot-water tap, turn on sufficient cold water to cover the tubing resting in the bottom of the bath ; then add the hot water, and there will be no steam worth mentioning.

378. **Tarnished Silver** can be quickly cleaned with a cloth sprinkled with bicarbonate of soda.

379. **To Take the Smell of Paint from a Room.**—Get a large bunch of hay and sprinkle with chloride of lime. Close windows and doors and leave closed for several hours, or overnight. The ill-effects of the poison in fresh paint are thus carried right away by the lime.

380. **When Whitewashing,** add a handful or two of salt to the whitewash. This makes it stick and there will be no " drippings."

381. **To Clean a Frying-pan.**—The dirtiest frying-pan will come clean if soaked for a few minutes in ammonia and water.

382. **A Saucepan Hint.**—A good idea when buying new saucepans is to buy at the same time a round enamel dish to fit in the saucepan at the top. The lid does for both. In the saucepan you can cook your vegetables and in the dish steam fish or steak or chops, tomatoes or any pudding left from the day before. Saves a gas jet and a separate pan.

383. **A Good Hint for the Dish-washing.**—If the family is a large one, collect your cups and saucers, small bread plates together. As you wash them turn upside down in a strong wicker basket (a good-sized waste paper basket is the thing as it can be picked up and put in the pantry or anywhere out of sight). The things just dry themselves.

384. **A Knitting Hint.** In knitting stockings, when you get to the heel put half the stitches on to a safety pin and continue knitting the bottom half of the foot, after you have done the heel. Next do the top half of the foot, and then seam neatly up the sides. When the stockings need re-footing, unpick the seams and just knit the heel and underfoot. The top of the foot seldom wears. If stockings are of silk or Sylko, etc., it is impossible to tell they have been re-footed as the new part is underneath the shoe.

385. **A Use for Sour Milk.**—Put sour milk in a pan and warm. Pour off all the " whey " and the curds can then be made into cream cheese by adding a piece of butter and pepper and salt, or be made into a curd cheese-cake by adding sugar, small piece of butter, nutmeg and a few currants.

386. **To Clean Sponges.**—Wash out sponges with ammonia, then in water in which is cream of tartar. Rinse in clear water and dry in the sun.

387. **Frying Pan—To clean.**—Make your frying pan as smooth and shiny as new by scouring it with powdered Bristol brick and a piece of lemon.

388. **To Prevent Salt Lumps in Shaker.**—A few grains of rice in your salt-shaker will prevent the forming of lumps.

389. **To Prevent Pudding Sticking to Cloth.**—To turn out a pudding boiled in a basin, hold it for a few moments in cold water. This will prevent it sticking to the cloth.

390. **To avoid the taste of unpleasant Medicine.**—Eat a peppermint toffee just before taking medicine and you will not taste the medicine, however nasty.

391. **An Improved Hay-Box Cooker.**—Buy a "Tate" sugar box from grocer, and half truss of hay. Line box with newspaper to ensure it being air-tight. Fix the lid of box with hinges and a hasp and staple to fasten. Make a cushion of a little of the hay, utilising the sack it was bought in. Then pack rest in box as tightly as possible, leaving room for one (or two) saucepans, over which the cushion will go. Vegetables, stews, porridge, etc., once brought to the boil and quickly placed in hay-box will cook without fear of burning or being overdone. Approximately double the time for cooking should be allowed. On top of box nail a smaller one, in which can be stored preservene soap, and on top of this nail an old piece of lino. This, being washable, if placed next to the sink, makes a convenient receptacle for dishes, etc., both before and after washing-up.

392. **Cure for Ear-ache.**—Warm a few drops of glycerine and drop into the ear.

393. **Cold Tea-leaves,** bound on a burn, take the pain away at once.

394. **To Kill Bugs.**—Spirits of Naphtha rubbed with a small painter's brush into every part of a bedstead is a *certain* way of getting rid of bugs. The mattress and bedding should be examined, and the same process performed, as they generally harbour more in these parts than in the bedstead.

395. **How to Test Eggs.**—Fill a basin with water and put the eggs in one by one. A fresh egg sinks to the bottom and lies flat ; if it rises slightly it is not perfectly fresh, and if it floats it is bad.

396. **Pickles should be Crisp.**—To make pickles crisp, a piece of alum the size of a filbert should be added to the vinegar used for pickling.

397. **Gum Water for Stiffening Linen.**—Dissolve two ounces of gum arabic in a pint of hot water, use it in proportion of two tablespoonfuls to two quarts of water.

398. **Sweet-smelling Clothes.**—A small piece of orris root placed in the copper will impart a lasting fragrance to the clean linen.

399. **To Remove Stains of any description.**—Soak the article in a solution of " hypo," which is used for fixing photographs and which can be bought at any chemist's. Then wash the article with preservene soap. This method has been known to remove such stains as those caused by iodine, ink, etc.

400. **Oil of Eucalyptus Removes Most Stains.**—It is not generally known that when stains of almost any description get on cloth, or velvet, or any delicate material, that oil of Eucalyptus will quickly remove all stain and leave no mark. I have never known this to fail when rubbed on with a small piece of clean linen.

401. **Washing Hint.**—Before washing a coloured table cloth or anything equally large, which has been stained, it is a good plan to sew round the stains with large tacking threads, because when the cloth is once immersed in the water the stains are difficult to see, but can be easily rubbed when they are located.

402. **No More Iron-mould Stains.**—If the inside of your copper makes ironmould marks on the washing try this remedy. Get a child's wooden hoop, one larger than the size of your copper, and enough calico to make a bag that will fit comfortably inside the copper, and sew this on to the hoop. When you boil the clothes, fit this inside the copper and put your clothes into it. You will never have any more copper-stained linen.

403. **A Cake Hint.**—A cake can be baked most successfully in a sweet tin with the cover on. First make two small holes in the cover with a nail. Grease tin and half fill with cake mixture. Do not take cover off until the cake is nearly done. A cake can be baked in this way at the same time as roasting a joint, as it will not go flat through opening the oven door.

404. **To Keep the Works of a Watch Clean.**—Cut a piece of white paper to the size of the cover, and, after soaking the paper in petrol, or paraffin, place it within the inner case. The paper should be periodically removed and a fresh piece, also soaked in petrol, or paraffin, substituted.

405. **To Mend a Cracked Bottle.**—Get some waterglass in syrup form, such as that commonly employed to preserve eggs. Make the bottle very hot by leaving it in an oven or in front of a fire. Put in the cork closely and then paint all over the outside of the crack with waterglass. Place the bottle on one side, and as the air inside the bottle cools and contracts, the waterglass is drawn into the crack, so that it is completely closed. Leave for a few days and the bottle will then safely hold liquid.

406. **A Paint Tip.**—Get a 2 lb. tin of ordinary paint and a pennyworth of size. Dissolve the size in a pint of boiling water. Mix in the paint while the solution is hot. This paint will shine like enamel. It has the additional advantage of drying as it is being applied.

407. **A Stocking Ladder.**—When a hole or ladder is found in a silk or lisle stocking and a needle and cotton is not obtainable, rub in a little soap above and below the hole. This saves a ladder going all down the stocking.

408. **A Pantry Hint.**—Take a piece of coarse meshed calico a little larger than the window, and dye it dark green.

When dry pin on to window frame by means of drawing pins. The window can then be kept wide open with no fear of cats intruding or smuts blowing in, as is the case when wire gauze is used.

409. **A Most Excellent Home-made Corn Cure.** Get an ordinary swede. Cut and dig out a hole in the top. Fill hole with common salt, and allow to stand until dissolved. Soften the corn morning and night with this liquid. In a few days you will be able to take out the whole corn by the roots.

410. **A Clothes Hanging Hint.**—If very cold before hanging out clothes, place the pegs in the oven and heat them. This will keep the hands pleasantly warm while pegging on the wire.

411. **That Useful Safety Pin.**—A large safety pin is a very useful holder for odd buttons, and loose hooks and eyes. Slip in the buttons, hooks and eyes, and close the pin, and you have everything handy.

412. **To Ease Corns.**—Take a small piece of tissue paper and wrap same round the toe having the corn. This will form a cushion and be found most beneficial.

413. **To Restore a Slimy Sponge.**—Obtain half a basin of fairly hot water and in it put about two pennyworth of salts of lemon (purchased from any chemist). Immerse slimy sponge several times, squeezing same after each immersion. It will be found that after several immersions the sponge will be quite clean and all sliminess will have disappeared. Finally rinse in clear warm water and sponge will be as good as new.

414. **To Make Colours " Fast."**—When washing a material containing several colours, pour two or three drops of blue-black ink into the water. By so doing it will prevent the colours from " running."

415. **To Sharpen Scissors.**—A good way to sharpen scissors is to use them on the neck of a bottle as if you were trying to cut the neck off. Do this until they are sharp enough.

416. **To Clean a Clock.**—Put a piece of cloth that has been steeped in paraffin oil in the bottom of the clock. The fumes will go up and clean away all dust and dirt and afterwards it will be found that the clock will go all right.

417. **Aluminium Saucepans.**—Everyone who uses aluminium saucepans knows how difficult it is to keep them free from the dark stain that collects inside, and what labour it is to remove it. Just boil some rhubarb or rhubarb leaves in the stained pan and it will become beautifully clean and white. When rhubarb cannot be obtained vinegar will do nearly as well and can be used several times over. The outside blackness can at once be removed by washing with preservene soap, which makes the pan like new.

418. **A Splendid and Cheap Night-Light** may be made by getting a ¼ lb. empty cocoa tin, and with a skewer make a small hole in the lid. Fill the tin with cotton wool, pour in a small quantity of paraffin, push a little bit of cotton wool through the hole in the lid, replace lid, and you have a night-light that will burn for hours, only requiring a little paraffin nightly.

419. **Method in Ironing.**—When the wash is large iron as follows. Take towels, sheets, pillow cases, etc., lay them perfectly flat on the table, and leave them under the ironing sheet whilst the rest of the clothes are being ironed. The articles under the sheet will not then require separate ironing.

420. **Blueing Hint.**—A lump of soda dissolved in the blue water prevents the blue from marking the clothes.

421. **A Bread-cutting Hint.**—Before cutting new bread dip the knife into boiling water. By this means the thinnest slices of bread may be cut from a new loaf without trouble. When cutting bacon into rashers, warm the knife first and it will cut both easily and neatly.

422. **Saucepans—To clean.**—If a saucepan becomes burnt, simply fill with salt water and leave for twenty-four hours. It can then be readily cleansed.

423. **To Clean Gold or Tinsel Braid.**—Get some rock ammonia and pound it into a powder. Apply this to the gold or tinsel braid, and rub briskly. The tarnish will disappear at once.

424. **Make Old Bird like a Spring Chicken** by steaming two hours, then browning in hot oven.

425. **How to Make Inexpensive Jam or Pickle Covers.**—Save your greaseproof paper. Cut out the size of the jars you wish to cover. Pour a little milk into a basin or bowl, dip the paper into the milk and squeeze out. Spread over the jars, pressing all round. In a short time it will be quite airtight and hard and requires no tying.

426. **To Roast Without an Oven.**—Get two large enamel pie dishes, one slightly smaller than the other. Place fat in bottom, and when hot put in joint or poultry. Potatoes can also be cooked with them. Cover over with other pie dish as lid, on low gas jet. Turn meat occasionally. This roasts beautifully, requires little attention, saves oven gas and cleaning of same. Plates and dishes can be warmed on top.

427. **A Clothes' Sprinkler.**—Get a clean bottle with a tightly fitting cork, cut a groove in the side of the cork ; fill the bottle with water and put cork in. You will find this is a much cleaner and better method than the old way of using the hands. It is not so messy.

428. **The Quickest Cure for an Early Cold.**—Should a child have a chill, take a square of camphor and a piece of lard the same size. Rub the camphor on the lard, and rub the throat and chest well. Continue the operation until a nice glow is felt, and in the morning the little one will be quite fit again.

429. **A Novel Use for an Old Calendar.**—If a calendar seems too pretty to destroy, paste a piece of sandpaper on the calendar pad and use it as a match scratcher. One of these in each room will be very useful.

430. **White Socks with Coloured Border.**—During the summer the children's white socks get so dirty and stained and as many of them had coloured tops, I did not think it wise to boil them, and it took me ages to rub them clean. Now when boiling the clothes (which I do in a zinc bath) I tie a string from handle to handle and pin the socks to it, letting them into the water just as far as I wish by lowering the string. The same applies to anything white with coloured border.

431. **The Quickest Way to Remove a Small Blood-stain.**—Break off a length of ordinary white sewing cotton and hold it in the mouth for a second. Then take it out and squeeze it on the stain, and all trace of blood quickly disappears.

432. **A Work-Box Wrinkle.**—To save time in hunting for reels of cotton, which take up so much room in a workbox, thread them all on wire (ordinary cotton covered wire not string), and form into circle. They will run quite easily when a length is required, and every thickness and colour is at hand.

433. **To Remove Soot from Chimneys.**—To save having the sweep, make a bright fire and put an ounce of flowers of sulphur on. It will remove all the soot from chimney flues.

434. **Measuring Butter.**—Half a cupful of butter is given in many recipes. The quickest way to arrive at this is to fill the measuring cup half full of water, and then to drop in the butter until the water rises to the top. Drain this off and half a cupful of butter will remain. This takes far less time than to pack the butter down into the cup. It also saves butter, as none will be left sticking to the sides of the cup. Other fats can be measured in the same way.

435. **Blood-stains on Silk, Satins, Crepe de Chine, etc.**—can be easily removed by making a thick paste of starch and water and covering the stain with it. Leave till quite dry, then brush the starch off with soft brush and all signs of blood will have disappeared and no harm will be done to the material.

436. **To Clean a Mincing Machine.**—It is very difficult to dry the inside of a mincing machine. The best way to clean it after using is to grind stale pieces of bread through it. This will be found to collect all grease, fat and skin from the small knives. Wipe with a clean cloth.

437. **To Clean Knives.**—Take a piece of felt and sprinkle with a drop or two of methylated spirit and fine bathbrick. Roll round and work the knife in and out while pressing on tightly with the other hand. A good polish will result.

438. **To Put Out a Chimney Fire.**—If the chimney gets on fire, quickly put some wet newspapers on the fire. The steam will quickly put the chimney fire out.

439. **To Remove Stains from Brown Shoes.**—Wring out a soft cloth in warm water, rub it on a bar of preservene soap and thoroughly wash the stained parts of the shoe. Wipe over with cloth without any soap and leave in air to dry. When thoroughly dry, apply brown shoe polish

with soft rag, rubbing well into parts which have been washed and polish in usual way. For obstinate stains a second washing may be necessary, but in most cases one washing will completely remove them.

440. **To Fasten Oilcloth Securely.**—Make a paste as for wall paper, and paste on the table or shelves. Put on oilcloth and rub straight with a duster. This prevents any slipping about and does not damage the oilcloth like tintacks.

441. **Weights and Measures.**—Take a clean, empty tin, of as large a diameter as possible and preferably without the sides being turned inwards at the top. Mark inside with a scratch about one inch long where the tin has to be filled for $\frac{1}{4}$ lb. flour ; similarly for $\frac{1}{2}$ lb. flour, $\frac{1}{4}$ lb. sugar, $\frac{1}{2}$ lb. sugar, $\frac{1}{4}$ lb. currants and any other ingredients in constant use (e.g., for making cakes, scones, etc.). Each new line should be marked with the amount and name of the ingredient, either in full or with its initial letter or with a sign the user remembers. (The diameter of the tin should be as large as possible, so that one can see easily into the tin ; the sides should be straight for ease of pouring out.) A large-sized tumbler can be likewise marked with a glass-cutter's tool, and perhaps the marks are more easily read, but there is more risk of a break, which necessitates another tumbler being marked afresh. This is useful, economical and labour-saving because : (1) It does away with the use of scales where many articles are concerned ; (2) Where scales are used weights are often misplaced, and, if there are children, lost, as weights make good playthings ; (3) If, after losing weights one remembers that " a cupful of —— weighs —— ounces," this does not help much, as cups vary in size.; (4) In using scales one often puts too much in the pan and then there is trouble in taking some out again. With a tin marked as above it is easy to get the correct amount at once.

**442. To Make Woollens Moth-proof.**—Use a solution of 1 lb. of alum to four quarts of water. This will be found an absolute preventive against moths.

**443. Copper and Bath filling Hint for Washing Day.**—When washing and rinsing one often requires the water in copper replenished and many changes of clean water in small baths close handy. Instead of placing each receptacle under the tap it is merely necessary to place a trough under the tap and direct it to the articles to be filled. The housewife will readily see that the strain of lifting heavy baths and pails is considerably diminished. The trough is constructed with two pieces of wood nailed together at right angles.

**444. To Stop a Door Rattling.**—To remedy a rattling door, which can be very disturbing, especially during the night, cut a piece of cork the exact thickness required to make the door fit firmly when closed. Secure it to the door frame a little above the lock with glue or seccotine, afterwards painting to the same colour as the door, so that it will not be noticed.

**445. To Remove Red Ink-stains from Table Linen.**—Spread freshly-made mustard over the stain and leave for half an hour. Then sponge off, and all trace of the ink will have disappeared.

**446. Varnish may be Brightened** by rubbing it with a cloth moistened in linseed oil.

**447. To Prevent Silver Tarnishing.** A few pieces of camphor put into the drawer in which silver is kept will prevent the latter from becoming tarnished.

**448. To Restore Suede Shoes.**— A mixture of equal parts of olive oil and black ink will restore suede shoes and slippers and remove rustiness.

449. **Fowl, to make Tender.**—When boiling an old fowl or tough meat, add a pinch of soda to the water. Simmer gently and the meat will be tender.

450. **When Tying Down Jam-pot Covers,** damp the string. The knot will not slip in the process, and when dry the string will shrink and tighten.

451. **Bone knife Handles** which have become yellow, can be whitened by rubbing with a flannel moistened with a solution of peroxide of hydrogen and water.

452. **To Clean Paint Brushes.**—Heat some vinegar to boiling point, and allow the brush to simmer in it for half an hour. Then wash well in strong soap suds and the brush will be like new.

453. **To Freshen Black Cloth.**—Black cloth that shows signs of wear can be restored to almost its original freshness by scrubbing with a soft brush dipped in the water in which ivy leaves have been boiled until they are soft. An old saucepan should be used for this purpose as the liquid stains and this method is not to be recommended if there are any cuts or scratches on the hands. After scrubbing, the material should be rubbed with a dark, dry cloth, and hung out to dry.

454. **To Make a Candle Fit the Candlestick,** dip the end in hot water. It will then be soft enough to be moulded to the necessary size.

455. **An Egg Hint.**—Eggs covered with boiling water and allowed to stand for five minutes are more nourishing and more easily digested than eggs placed in boiling water and allowed to boil for three and a half minutes.

456. **Turning Out a Jelly.**—To turn out a jelly whole, grease the mould before pouring in the liquid. If this has not been done and you are afraid the jelly is not going

to turn out whole, plunge the mould into hot water and you will have no more trouble.

457. **Uses for Vinegar.**—Moisten the stove polish with a few drops of vinegar instead of cold water. Only a gentle rubbing will be needed afterwards to produce a bright polish. When eggs are scarce, add a dessertspoonful of vinegar and one egg to a large plain cake for which, without the vinegar, three eggs would be used. When boiling fish add a few drops of vinegar to the water ; the fish will then be quite firm and white. If an egg has a very thin shell, or is chipped and is likely to crack when boiled, add a few drops of vinegar to the water. Vinegar is useful for reviving colours. Add one teaspoonful of vinegar to each quart of cold rinsing water, wring tightly and dry quickly.

458. **Handy Kitchen Measures.**—A level breakfast-cupful of flour, cornflour or arrowroot, weight about ¼ lb. ; a breakfastcupful of breadcrumbs (pressed in), weighs about ¼ lb. ; a breakfastcupful of sago, tapioca, hominey (heaped), weighs about ¼ lb. ; a breakfastcupful of brown sugar (heaped), weighs about ½ lb. ; A breakfastcupful of castor sugar (heaped), weighs about 7 ozs. ; a breakfast-cupful of rice (heaped), weighs about 7 ozs. ; a breakfast-cupful of suet, chopped fine (heaped), weighs about ½ lb. ; a breakfastcupful of butter, lard, margarine or dripping (level), weighs about 7 ozs. ; A breakfastcupful of currants, sultanas, raisins (heaped), weighs about ½ lb. ; 10 sheets of leaf gelatine weighs about 1 oz. ; 1 heaped tablespoonful of flour weighs about 1 oz. ; 2 heaped tablespoonsful of breadcrumbs weigh about 1 oz. ; 1 level tablespoonful of demerara sugar weighs about 1 oz. ; 1 level tablespoonful of castor sugar weighs about 1 oz. ; 1 rounded tablespoonful of icing sugar weighs about 1 oz. ; 5 lumps of loaf sugar weigh about 1 oz. ; 2 tablespoonsful of liquid equal about 1 fluid oz. ; 1 teacupful of liquid equals about 1 gill.

459. **To Keep Mint Fresh,** wash it in water which carbonate of soda has been added, and when dry it will be quite green.

460. **Wrap Greens in Wet Cloth.**—All greens such as parsley, mint, celery, lettuce, if wrapped in a wet cloth, and rolled up will keep crisp and fresh.

461. **A Handy Peg-bag.**—Buy a penny coat-hanger, then make a bag of strong canvas, leaving about two inches open on both sides. Make a hem on one side of the bag over the coat-hanger, and hem the other side, leaving it hanging loose. Hang the hook on washing days on the clothes-line, with the pegs inside, and push the bag along as you require it. Then the pegs can be taken out without stooping, and many a backache is saved.

462. **In the Absence of a Wringer,** it will be found a good plan to have fixed up over the sink, or any other convenient place, a rod on two extending brackets, similar to that used for roller towels. Put the clothes over the rod and wring. It is surprising how dry the clothes can be wrung.

463. **To Make Tablecloths Last.**— A tablecloth will last nearly twice as long if, as soon as there is the slightest sign of wear, four inches are cut off one side and one end, and all hemmed again. This will bring the fold in a new place, as it is in the folds that a cloth usually wears first.

464. **To Save Sheets.**—By putting a piece of wide tape about six inches long, and stitching it at both ends round the corners of the sheets, they last much longer and do not tear, as is often the case when drying in windy weather.

465. **Stains on Carpets.**—Dry flour sprinkled and rubbed on carpets, and left for some hours will absorb grease or oil accidentally spilt.

466.  **To make Jam,** which will keep and be clear, keep stirring and don't skim it ;  the scum will disappear by itself.

467.  **To Loosen Articles that have become fixed.**—If glass stopper becomes fixed, tap round it with another ; if tumblers become fixed, gently tap with another ;  if two flower-pots are fixed, tap with another ;  two iron screws tap with piece of iron ;  and so on.  Always the rule—tap each article with one similar.

468.  **To Banish Cockroaches.**—If cockroaches and ants are troublesome in the house, sprinkle ground rice around their haunts.  They eat greedily and it swells inside them and they die.

469.  **To Test Tinned Fruit and Vegetables.**—Open the tin and plunge into its contents a bright steel knife.  Let it remain a few moments, when, if copper is present even in minute quantities, it will be visibly deposited on the blade.  This is an unfailing test.

470.  **Clean Jam Jars.**—Don't put jam into jars that have had fat in ;  it will not keep, however much the jar may have been washed.

471.  **Iron-holders.**—Tops of leather boots and old soft gloves tacked together and rounded make excellent iron holders, and saves burning hands.

472.  **To Mend Cracks in Ceiling before re-Whitewashing.** Take lengths of 2-inch bandage of calico and dip them in paste.  Put them one at a time, alternate ways, till a square is formed to cover the crack or hole.  Press each well to the ceiling before putting the next one across.  When all are quite dry, whitewash over and the crack will be quite unnoticeable.

473.  **To Remove Paint from Glass** try a safety-razor blade.

474. **When Washing Silk Blouses** add a tablespoonful of starch or borax and half a teaspoonful of turpentine to the rinsing water. The blouse will then iron up equal to new.

475. **To Stop Hiccoughs.**—A lump of sugar saturated with vinegar will stop hiccoughs.

476. **When Machining** cotton goods. Keep a piece of preservene soap handy, to rub along the seams to be sewn. This ensures you a quick easy run, without the fear of breaking cotton.

477. **A Novel Kindler.**—Potato peelings thoroughly dried in a cool oven make very good firelighters instead of wood, and burn up very quickly.

478. **To Mend Torn Umbrella.**—A neat and novel way to mend a torn umbrella, if the rent is not too large, is to stitch firmly a piece of black court plaster on the inside. This does not show nearly as much as a darn.

479. **To Soften Water.**—To soften water, put squeezed lemons, or the peel of oranges into the jug on the washstand. They will soften the water equal to rain water, and impart an agreeable perfume to it.

480. **Flowers** will be found to have a richer, deeper colour if soot water is given to the plants at intervals.

481. **Rancid Butter** can be restored to freshness if broken up into small pieces, and put into a bowl of new milk. Let it remain there for an hour, then drain. Wash in cold salted water, and form into pats again.

482. **A Cake Hint. To prevent the bottom of your cake from burning** stand the tin on a tray of sand or ashes.

483. **To Clean Ostrich Feathers,** draw the feather very gently through the losely closed hand from base to tip in strong lukewarm suds of preservene soap. Rinse in clear lukewarm water. For white feathers add a little blue. Tie a piece of string to the end of the quill ; hang to dry. Shake while drying. If only loose curl is wanted, shake the feather over a warm stove. If tight curl desired, curl each tiny feather with a silver fruit knife, running it along feather.

484. **To Clean Rattan, Reed, or Willow Furniture.—** First remove the dust by blowing with bellows or a bicycle pump, then wash with warm soapsuds made with preservene soap. Apply with a scrubbing-brush and wipe with cloth. Set in sun to dry if possible.

485. **Hearthstones.—**Clean with hot water, then apply hearthstone with thin starch, which makes it last longer.

486. **To Stitch Heavy Fabrics,** such as heavy duck or canvas, rub the hems and seams with soap and the needle will easily penetrate.

487. **The best way to make a Cushion** is to cut the cloth on the cross. Line the cover, when made with wadding, and then fill it with down.

488. **To ease an insect bite** apply strong carbolic ointment or liquid ammonia just on the bite.

489. **For a Burn.—**Charcoal laid flat while cold on a burn causes pain to abate immediately. By leaving it on for an hour the burn seems almost healed. This applies to superficial burns.

490. **Put New Pie-dishes and Pudding-bowls** in pan of cold water and bring to boil. Allow to get cold in same water before using. They will last three times as long.

491. **An Ironing Hint.**—If the ironing sheet wrinkles up when ironing, place a folded newspaper underneath.

492. **To Clean Knives** quickly, rub with large cork dipped in water and then in plate powder.

493. **To Clean Lamp Burners,** wash or boil in water in which beans have been cooked. Stand on stove to dry.

494. **Prepare New Baking Tins** by placing in oven with thick layer of bran in them till bran is dry. Puddings, cakes, etc., will then never stick.

495. **To whiten Poached Eggs** drop a little vinegar into the water.

496. **To Wash Shetland Shawls.**—Squeeze them in two soapy lathers of preservene soap. To the rinsing water add thick made starch in proportion of 1 tablespoonful starch to 1½ gallons of water and a little blue. Do not wring, but squeeze. Fold in towel, beat with hands till nearly dry. Lay on sheet on floor, cut four equal pieces of tape exact size of shawl, pin these on sheet where four sides of shawl should come to and pin carefully through the tape to sheet. Leave to dry.

497. **To Wash Chiffon.**—Place chiffon in a large bowl filled with tepid suds of preservene soap. Move about in the water and press gently between the hands, but do not rub. Pour off the water and thoroughly rinse. Take the entire piece of fabric between the hands at once, and lay on a thick turkish towel. Pull into shape, cover with a second towel and roll up. Press with a warm (not hot) iron while still damp.

498. **To make your own Smelling Salts.**—Put some small lumps of rock ammonia into a bottle. Cover the rock ammonia with eau de Cologne and cork tightly.

499. **Irons—The care of.**—Never let irons get red hot or hang about on range. Spoils temper and they will never afterwards retain heat so well.

500. **Lines and Pegs.**—Always boil new clothes' lines and pegs ten minutes before using.

501. **Cover all Shelves in Cupboards with thin Oilcloth** nailed down. If wiped over with a cloth wrung out in preservene soapsuds shelves are always clean as new.

502. **To Destroy Moths** in infested carpets. Go over entire surface systematically with a hot iron, pressing over a cloth wrung out of cold water, not too dry. The steam will kill both eggs and larvæ.

503. **To Wash Knitted Garments.**—Free garment from all dust, then measure and write down the length and width of the front and back, length of shoulder and sleeves. Dissolve half a cake of preservene soap in three pints of water, simmer till all is dissolved, stir into a gallon of warm water. Put garment in and wash by lifting up and down and squeezing in soapy water. Take care not to stretch. Do not rub. Rinse in several warm waters. Squeeze between the hands ; roll in Turkish towel and squeeze as dry as possible. Set a table outdoors in the shade, cover with sheet. On this lay garment, with back next sheet. Draw points together and the sleeves straight out. Verify all measurements and if necessary stretch and pin the garment into shape. When partly dry turn the other side up.

504. **Flush all Lavatories** once a week with boiling water and strong preservene soapsuds, then they will always be sweet and clean.

505. **To Clean Lace.**—To wash real lace, place face down on a piece of clean white canvas material, taking care to

catch every point. Drive two stakes into the ground and nail crosspiece from one to the other. Over this lay the canvas lace up, like a tent, and fasten four corners canvas by means of strings to four pegs in the ground. With a soft shaving brush cover the lace with a very thick creamy lather of preservene soap. Allow to remain a few minutes, then before it dries rinse off by pouring clear lukewarm water over the surface. Continue rinsing till all soap is removed. Add a little blue to final water. Then sponge a thin solution of gum arabic, 1 oz. powdered gum arabic dissolved in one cupful boiling water. When canvas is nearly dry lay face down on Turkish towel and iron till entirely dry. Then carefully remove lace from canvas.

506. **Tan Shoes** that are badly soiled and spotted should be put on shoe trees and washed with flannel squeezed out of strong preservene soapsuds. Absorb as much moisture as possible by pressing with a handful of soft rags. Leave to dry. While still damp, rub in a little castor oil and when thoroughly dry polish as usual.

507. **Care of Wooden Utensils.**—The proper method is to wash and dry them as quickly as possible, using warm preservene soapsuds. Every now and then scrub with fine sands. This will keep them very white.

508. **To Clean Zinc.**—Scrub with warm water and preservene soap and a little vinegar. Rinse, and wipe dry. Then polish with a greased cloth.

509. **To Wash Eiderdown Quilts.**—Make a generous lather of preservene soap in enough warm water to cover quilt and soak for half an hour. Press the dirt out with a wooden mallet. Do not rub or wring. Rinse in same manner. Hang on line to drip and shake often. When partly dry beat lightly with a rattan carpet-beater to lighten the filling. Repeat several times.

510. **To Give Double Life to a Carpet.**—Where traffic is most, tack a broad band of webbing round the under border.

511. **To Clean a Panama Hat like new.**—Melt a little preservene soap and a little ammonia in water. A little glycerine added to the rinsing water makes it soft and flexible.

512. **Never put Loose Coal on Fire without damping it.**—If damped it will cake into hard lump and last well.

513. **To Make an Ebony Stain.**—With $\frac{1}{2}$ a pint of Spirit Black mix about $\frac{1}{2}$ a pint of methylated spirit. To this add a small quantity of flaked shellac. The shellac will give the stain a varnished surface. It is advisable not to put all the methylated spirit in at once, but to add in small quantities till the depth of tone required is obtained.

514. **Remove Creases from Silk Blouse.** When a silk blouse has become creased, from wearing under a coat, hang before a hot fire and the creases will drop out.

515. **Steamy Windows** can be remedied by applying a small quantity of glycerine with a soft clean rag after thoroughly washing and polishing in the ordinary way.

516. **To Disperse Ants.**—When ants come, if powdered borax is sprinkled over the spot they disappear entirely in a few hours.

517. **Before removing a new gas mantle from the box,** pass a thread through the loop on the top. Withdraw the mantle carefully, and then immerse it entirely in a glass of vinegar, leaving only the thread, the two ends of which should be tied together outside. Allow the mantle to remain in the vinegar for a minute or two, lift out and hang to dry. Place on the burner fork and burn off in the ordinary way. Treated in this way they last longer, are stronger and give a more brilliant light.

518.  **To make Celluloid Collars look like new** rub them lighty with a damp piece of flannel dipped in a little dry carbonate of soda, rinse well and polish with a soft cloth.

519.  **If your Milk Pudding gets burnt** remove the burnt skin, add some more milk and a little butter, and rebake in a gentle oven.

520.  **If you have an Iron Bedstead without a castor** get a thick rubber heel and jam the spike well into the rubber.  You will then have a nice flat surface for the bedstead to rest upon and you will save the wear and tear of the carpet

521.  **Uses of Potato.**—Cold potatoes used instead of soap cleanse the hands well, and make the skin soft and smooth.  The water in which potatoes have been boiled is excellent for sponging dirt out of silk.  Potato water made by grating a potato into half a pint of cold water and afterwards straining it is splendid for cleaning cloth and serge skirts from which it will remove even obstinate mud stains.

522.  **An easy way of picking Red or Black Currants,** is to pull them through an ordinary table fork.  This is a much quicker way, and it keeps the hands free from stains.

523.  **To preserve Roses for Winter,** pick them just before they are in full bloom, making sure that the stem is broken off from the thick stem of the tree.  Then melt some ordinary sealing wax and wrap the ends of the stems in it. Roll in tissue paper and place in an air tight tin or box. When you want roses take them out, in the evening if possible, cut off the waxed ends, and leave in water over night.  Next day the roses will be found to have bloomed and to be as perfect as if only just picked.

524. **Old shabby Patent Shoes** can be renovated by applying black spirit enamel with a small paint brush. Two coatings will make a new pair of shoes.

525. **To Save Polish.**—If the flannel cloth that is used to put the metal polish on is kept in a tightly closed tin, it will not be necesssary to use polish every time, thus making a tin of polish last twice as long.

526. **To keep the edge of a Carpet or Mat from Curling up,** make some very thick starch and paste it along the edge. Then get an iron which is fairly hot, place some brown paper over the starched part and dry it with the iron.

527. **Ironing Blanket Substitute.**—An excellent substitute for an ironing blanket is to get about half a dozen newspapers ; spread them out flat and smooth and fix them together by a few stitches at each corner. This will retain the heat of the iron longer than a blanket. A folded newspaper is much better than a duster for " trying the iron." It cleans the iron and makes it beautifully smooth.

528. **A good Cold Cure** is to pour half a pint of boiling milk on to a heaped teaspoonful of ground Cinnamon. Sweeten to taste and stir well. Sip this in bed as hot as possible and your cold will be cured.

529. **An Easy Way to Copy Embroidery** from any material is to place a piece of paper over the embroidery and rub over well with the back of a spoon. A reproduction of the design will appear on the paper in a very short time.

530. **When Corset Steels work out** of the casing instead of sewing the end again, pull the steels out several inches, smear them over with seccotine then replace them and press the casing so that it adheres firmly. There will be no more trouble with the steels.

531. **Beetles, Cockroaches, Crickets** and other household pests may be quite cleared in a fortnight by the use of borax. Put this in a tin box which has a perforated lid and sprinkle it round sinks, grates, over the kitchen floor and scullery floor, and wherever the pests have been noticed. Renew the borax every two or three days.

532. **Coffee Grounds,** like tea leaves, may be sprinkled on the floor to prevent dust rising while sweeping.

533. **To Dry Clothes in Frosty Weather.**—If a handful of common salt is added to the rinsing water, clothes hung to dry in the garden will not freeze.

534. **To remove burnt taste from Milk.**—Place the jug into a pan of cold water, add a pinch of salt and stir well.

535. **Cracks in Unseasoned Wood.**—Cracks sometimes occur in articles made of unseasoned wood. Hide the cracks by filling them with bees-wax melted sufficiently to make it pliable. Smooth the surface and sand paper the surrounding part, collecting the dust formed and working it into the bees-wax in the crack. Stain and the crack will scarcely be noticeable.

536. **A Wet Oven Cloth** saves many burnt fingers and hands.

537. **To Renovate Oil-Cloth.**—Turpentine mixed with warm milk makes oilcloth look like new.

538. **Black Cloth that Shows Signs of Wear** can be restored to almost its original freshness by scrubbing with a soft brush dipped in the water in which ivy leaves have been boiled until they are soft. An old saucepan should be used for this purpose as the liquid stains, and this method is not to be recommended if there are any cuts or scratches on the hands. After scrubbing, the material should be rubbed with a dry, dark cloth and hung out to dry.

539. **Mahogany** should be washed with vinegar or cold tea.

540. **Clean Walnut Furniture** with a flannel dipped in paraffin.

541. **Spots of Milk or Tea on a Brass Tray** will vanish with an application of lemon-juice.

542. **Clean Gas-Stove Burners once a week.**—Pierce the holes with a hat-pin and scour the ring in hot water and soda.

543. **A Stocking Hint.**—When stockings are new, and each time they come from the laundry, rub the threads of the heels and toes thoroughly on the right side with a piece of bees-wax. This will lengthen the life of the fine lisle and cotton hose greatly.

544. **For a Tagel Hat,** the crown of which has developed a point through being wet ; while the hat is still damp fill a pound jam jar with boiling water and placing the hat crown downwards on a table, stand the jar in the crown. Leave for some hours and upon removal the crown will be found to be as flat as when new.

545. **Uses of Starch.**—Powered Starch is an excellent silver polish and it removes stains from wallpaper when nothing else will, while if, when washing windows, a lump of starch is added to the water the dirt will be removed more easily.

546. **A little Vinegar added to Stewed Prunes** greatly improves the flavour. Although it may seem strange it causes less sugar to be used.

547. **To Keep Shop Windows from Steaming** wash them perfectly clean and thoroughly polish them, then apply a soft clean rag moistened with a small quantity of glycerine.

548. **To Renovate Silver Embroidery** worked on white satin take some cream of tartar or powered magnesia and rub it well into the embroidery with a stiff nail or tooth brush. Take care not to rub the satin. The tarnish will soon disappear.

549. **To Drive a Nail in a Wall.**—When a wall is soft and loose and a nail will not bear the weight of a picture, mix a little plaster of Paris with some water. Scoop out a small hole in the wall, fill it in with plaster, insert the nail gently. The plaster will harden in a minute or two.

550. **To Break Eggs.**—To those who find separating eggs a difficulty a simple method is to break the egg into a funnel ; the white then runs through, the yolk remains.

551. **When Polishing the Kitchen Range,** add a few drops of vinegar to the blacking. It gives a brighter gloss and stays on longer.

552. **Drying Coloured Frocks.**—Coloured frocks should never be hung out to dry in bright sunlight. Hang them in a shady place. Take care the irons are not too hot when ironing them, as too great a heat will fade the colours quickly. Blues and lavenders are particularly susceptible to sun and heat.

553. **Washing Babies' Woollies.**—One of the greatest difficulties in washing babies' woollies is wringing without pulling them out of shape. Put an ordinary enamel colander into the bowl in which the article is to be washed. Drop the wet jacket, frock, etc., into this and knead very firmly. This gives a firm surface to squeeze against, and the holes let the water run away freely. When clean give a final rinsing in clean soapy water˙ This keeps the garment soft. Squeeze as dry as possible through the colander, spread out carefully on a flat surface,

arranging it in its proper shape (without stretching). Lay this out of doors if possible. Turn now and again while drying.

554. **The Best Iron stand.**—One of the best iron stands one can have is an ordinary brick heated. It holds the heat, and does not cool the iron as quickly as the ordinary stand.

555. **Paraffin Oil for Rheumatism.**—Well rubbed in, it will often ease the complaint.

556. **An Enamel Sheet for Table.**—A very useful utensil for the kitchen table is an enamel sheet, such as is supplied for the top of gas stoves. This will serve instead of a pastry board, and can be easily washed and dried. It is very serviceable for preparing vegetables and fruit, and does away with the scrubbing that boards require.

557. **A Leaky Saucepan.**—An ordinary patent fastener (dress) will save the situation if you suddenly discover a leak in a saucepan, or in fact, any kitchen utensil. Simply put one part of fastener each side of saucepan and press firmly till closed. The leak is thus mended temporarily until you can procure an ordinary leak stop.

558. **A Kettle Lid Hint.**—When the knob comes off the kettle lid, replace it with a cork. Cut the top off a medicine bottle cork, put a screw through the hole in the lid from the underneath, and screw the cork on to it. This makes a knob that is cool to hold.

559. **Nails on which Dishcloths, Mops, etc., hang,** often get rusty and unsightly. Give them three coats of white enamel, each being allowed to dry before the next is put on. This prevents any rust marks getting on the cloths.

560. **A Vegetable Cooking Suggestion.**—Cabbages and other greenstuffs need a lot of draining after cooking. Tie the greenstuff in coarse muslin before putting into the pan. When done, lift out the muslin bag with a fork or skewer, empty the water from the pan and then let the cabbage drain into the pan, suspending the bag from a skewer placed across the top of the pan. Keep the pan on the side of the stove, so that the cabbage does not cool. By the time the rest of the dinner is dished up the greenstuff will need very little pressing to make it quite dry.

561. **To Cook a Full Dinner in One Pan.**—Into a large saucepan place three or four jam jars, in which put stew, fish, rice, fruit, etc., covering each with greaseproof paper. The boiling water should come about two thirds of the way up the sides of the jars. Potatoes can be boiled in the water. In this way a whole meal can be cooked over one gas-ring. Keep the pan tightly covered.

562. **A Good Substitute for a Dutch Oven** can be made by turning a seven-pound biscuit tin on its side, with the opening towards the fire. The heat quickly concentrates inside the tin, and a hot oven is formed in which anything may be baked or heated without extra fuel. Plates may be heated by standing on the top.

563. **To Keep Meat Sweet in Hot Weather.**—Hang up in the meat safe muslin bags filled with fresh charcoal on each side of a joint of meat. This will keep the meat sweet even in the hottest weather.

564. **To Prevent Rust in Coppers.**—The complaint is often heard that wash house coppers rust and iron mould the clothes. This can be easily prevented by rubbing the boiler as soon as empty and while still warm with preservene soap. This should be done thoroughly until the boiler has a good coating of soap all over.

**565. To Restore Shrunken Flannel to its Normal Size.**—Try laying the article to be restored on the ironing board and on it spread a piece of cheese cloth which has been wrung out in cold water. Press with a hot iron until the cheese cloth is perfectly dry. The garment will show a decided improvement.

**566. To Polish Aluminium.**—The best way of cleaning and polishing aluminium utensils is first to remove the grease with pumice stone and then polish with rouge mixed with turpentine.

**567. Headache Cure.**—A wonderful cure for a bad headache is two cloves in a cup of freshly made tea.

**568. Soot will remove Grease Spots from Shoes.**

**569. Home-made Furniture Polish.**—A good furniture polish is made from 1 pint vinegar, 6d. turpentine and 2 eggs. Put half the vinegar and turpentine in a bottle and shake well, adding the beaten eggs. Shake the bottle for fifteen minutes when the mixture should be creamy, then add the other half of vinegar and turps. It should now be a thick cream and will provide a most excellent polish.

**570. A Cinder Sifter** which saves time, trouble and dust. Under the grate (when building) leave a hollow pit about 12 inches to 18 inches across and from 2 feet to 3 feet deep. Instead of tiles, cover with iron plates in which large holes have been bored. This plate being under the grate will not be seen. It should be left loose so that when pit is filled the cinders can easily be removed, or better still have a tin to fit cavity as this is easily taken out and replaced.

**571. To Wash Chintz or Cretonne,** and preserve their colours and gloss, take two lbs. of rice and boil it in two gallons of water till soft ; pour it into a tub ; let it stand until about the warmth generally approved for coloured linen ; then put the chintz in and use the rice instead of soap, then boil the same quantity of rice again, but strain the rice from the water, and mix it in warm clear water. Wash article in this till quite clean, afterwards rinse it in the water the rice was boiled in and this will answer better than starch.

572.  **To Whiten Linen or Calico.**—When linen has turned yellow from not being used cut up a pound of fine soap into a gallon of milk, and hang it over a fire in a wash kettle.  When the soap has completely melted put in the linen and boil it half an hour.  Then take it out ; have ready a lather of soap and water, wash the linen in it, and rinse through two cold waters, with a very little blue in the last.

573.  **To "Blanch" Almonds (removing skin).**—The quickest way is to put in a pan of cold water and bring to the boil.  Then drop immediately into *cold* water.  The skins can be removed by just rubbing with the finger.

574.  **Hints on First Aid.**

If poisoned, take of mustard, a tablespoon,
In a cup of warm water, and swallow right soon.
For burns try borax, and a wet bandage too ;
If blistered, then oil and dry flannel will do.
For children's convulsions, warm baths are the rule
With castor-oil dose, but keep the head cool.
Give syrup of ipecac when croup is in store.
For fainting stretch patient right flat on the floor
To soak in hot water is best for a sprain.
Remember these rules, and 'twill save you much pain.

575.  **To Clean Straw Hats.**—Put a teaspoonful of flowers of sulphur in a saucer and squeeze into it the juice of a lemon.  Apply this mixture to the hat with a nail brush, then rinse in cold water.  This method is both better and safer than oxalic acid.

576. **A Moth Preventive.**—The best preventive for moths is stone brimstone, broken into lumps, and scattered in boxes or drawers where furs and woollen articles are stored away. It rarely, if ever, fails. There is no odour perceptible, except by the moths, who very quickly recognise it.

577. **To Make Garments Non-inflammable.**—It is necessary in the interests of children that their clothing, especially flannelette, should be rinsed in water to which has been added 1 ounce of alum or sal-ammoniac which renders the material fireproof until washed again.

578. **Perfuming Lingerie.**—A small piece of orris root placed in the copper will impart a lasting fragrance to handkerchiefs and lingerie.

579. **Sand Paper Suede Shoes.**—If you want to clean a pair of suede shoes, black, gray or brown, rub them over with a sheet of sand-paper. Do not rub too hard. but use a firm, even pressure. All mud and grease will come off quickly.

580. **When Making Feather Pillows,** wax the inner covering and then the feathers will not be able to come through. To do this iron the wrong side of the tick with a hot flat-iron rubbed with beeswax, rubbing the iron over the wax each time before pressing on the cloth.

581. **A Bicycle Hint.**—A postage stamp will mend a puncture temporarily. A tube thus mended will keep up many miles. Do not blow up the inner tube until it is inside the outer tube.

582. **A Polish for Brown Leather.**—Beeswax dissolved in turpentine makes a good polish for brown leather.

583. **Salt Makes a good Tooth Cleaner.**—It hardens the gums and makes the teeth white.

584. **If a Casserole gets cracked and leaks** make a mixture of pea flour and water and let it stew all day by the fire. The pea flour will then get into the crack and stop the leak.

585. **Never Polish Pewter,** it spoils it and wears off the touch marks. Let pewter remain dull, when dirty take a soft brush and wash with warm water and a little soap then dry with a clean cloth.

586. **To Stiffen Thin Cotton Fabrics.**—Most women stiffen thin cotton fabrics by dissolving a few knobs of sugar in the rinse water, but the better way is to rinse the articles in a little borax water. This gives just the required stiffness, and there is no fear of any undissolved particle sticking to the iron.

587. **Bicycle Tubes are Useful.**—Flat lengths of inner tube neatly tacked along the bend of stairs, where linoleum is so apt to crack give fresh life to the material and do not look unsightly. Short lengths of old tyre are much better for training climbers than cloth and for binding between fruit trees and roses to keep the stakes from rubbing the trees. Small discs of old rubber tyres will mend a hole in a tennis shoe and a broad piece gummed across a rubber shoe will hold the sole together for a long time.

588. **Instead of Buying New Curtain Rings** and hooks, cover the old discoloured with vinegar and a little water boil them for a few minutes and then polish with a dry cloth.

589. **To Restore the Colour of Black Kid Boots,** apply with a sponge a mixture of one spoonful of sweet oil to two spoonfuls of black ink. Leave this on for a day then polish.

590. **To Preserve Eggs.**—If you put eggs into boiling water for one minute they will keep fresh for a month. Eggs will keep for six months if steeped for a little while in sweet oil.

591. **A Handy Weight.**—If a weight is needed to press anything down, place a bucket of water on a board over the article, one gallon of water weighs eight pounds.

592. **To Remove Sunburn.**—Lemon-juice mixed with milk removes sunburn. Pour half a cupful of hot milk on a slice of lemon, leave it for an hour or so, and then strain the mixture. Throw away the curd and use the clear liquid that remains.

593. **Hot Flannels.** Should hot flannels be wanted in the case of illness fill a hot water bottle with very hot water, and wind the flannels round it. This will heat them quickly and evenly, and will save holding them before a fire.

594. **To Prevent Salt from Lumping.**—Mix with corn-flour, one teaspoon corn-flour to six teaspoons salt.

595. **To Prevent Rugs from Curling.**—Sew to the underside of each corner a triangular piece of corrugated rubber in which holes have been punched to permit the passage of the needle.

596. **To Re-finish the Worn Edges of a Rug.**—When the edges of a rug become worn they can be refinished by button-holing with heavy yarn of the proper colour. A good looking finish can also be produced by holding a heavy blind cord along the worn edge and working over and over it with the yarn.

597. **To Measure Treacle Quickly.**—Dip the measuring cup or spoon in scalding water and the treacle will turn out quickly.

598. **A Good China Cement.**—One of the best cements for mending toilet ware and heavy bowls is made this way. Put an oyster shell into a bright fire and leave it there until it glows with heat. Take it out with a pair of tongs and put it on one side to cool. Then crush it to a fine powder and if possible pass it through a sieve. Mix the white dust into a paste with white of an egg and use this to join the fractured parts. Allow several days for the mended part to set and a very perfect union will be secured.

599. **To Make Earthenware Vessels and Casseroles Last.**—When new rub outside with a raw onion. This will prevent the vessel sweating and lessen contraction which is the cause of cracking when the pot is heated.

600. **To Straighten Celluloid Knitting Needles.**—Celluloid knitting needles often become bent. When this occurs pour hot water over them or hold in the steam from a kettle and straighten with the fingers. Then plunge into cold water to harden.

601. **To Remove Scratches and Polish Ebonized Furniture**—Paint with Indian ink. Smooth with fine sandpaper and paint again. When dry smear over with linseed oil when this has soaked in, polish with beeswax and turpentine.

602. **To Improve Oven for Baking.**—Whitewash the inside of an oven which will not bake well and the defect will be remedied.

603. **To Clean Kid Gloves.**—Have ready a little milk in a saucer and a piece of preservene soap. Spread out the glove on a clean cloth folded three or four times. Take a piece of flannel, dip in the milk, then rub off a good quantity of preservene soap and commence to rub the glove towards the fingers, holding it firmly. Continue this until the glove if white looks a dingy yellow. Lay it to dry and soon the soiled glove looks nearly new.

604. **New Brooms and Bannister Brushes** should have a fold of thick cloth, velvet or india-rubber nailed round them so that they do not chip or scratch the furniture. This saves much labour as work can be done quickly and well without the fear of leaving behind unsightly chips off the furniture or stairs.

605. **Turning Out a Cake.**—Often there is a little difficulty in turning out a cake from the tin, especially gingerbread. Much labour and trouble can be overcome by dredging a little flour over the greased tin before adding the mixture. Then after taking from the oven, stand the tin on a damp cloth for a minute or two and the cake will come out quite whole.

606. **When Storing Silk.**—When you want to put away a piece of silk for a blouse, do not put it away folded, or you will find it hopelessly crushed and soiled at the folds when you want to use it. Always roll silk rather loosely upon cardboard or a roll of newspaper wrapped in tissue paper. White silk or satin should have deep blue tissue paper wrapped outside to prevent it turning yellow.

607. **A Clothes Line Hint.**—This hint does away with line props which are apt to get blown down or get in the way of the washing. Into your line post screw two strong eyes, opposite each other, and pass the clothes line through them. Down the post screw in several hooks. When you want to raise the line, pull down the portion between the two screw eyes and fasten under one of the hooks.

608. **To Ease a Patient.**—When a patient has to lie down a great part of the day, great comfort is derived from the use of a firm pillow or cushion placed under the knees.

**609. A Homely Filter.**—A simple method of purifying water is to tie a small piece of clean undyed flannel on to the tap, leaving it rather loose, and it will be found to absorb all impurities. Renew the flannel from time to time.

**610. Butter as Ointment.**—Butter is found very useful in the home for sore lips, chapped hands, cuts, bruises of the skin, as the cream by which butter is made is such that even the worst bruise quickly vanishes after the first application.

**611. Grass versus Tea Leaves.**—People who use tea leaves when brushing their carpets will find that freshly cut grass gives better results.

**612. To Improve Brown Bread.**—Knead in with the whole wheat meal a well beaten egg. It prevents that crumbling so often found with brown bread and also improves the flavour.

**613. A Novel Floor Polisher.**—Not everyone has a mop to rub up the lino with, but everyone can get two bricks. Tie together and envelop with a piece of flannel or blanket. This is a splendid polisher and saves using strength.

**614. Shelling Eggs.**—Boiled eggs for salad. After boiling hard dip in cold water ; this keeps eggs a good colour. Roll between hands and soften shell, when it will be easily pulled off.

**615. To Clean Bead Lampshades.**—Take a small piece of preservene soap jelly, and with it make a lather with warm water. Dip the beads up and down, shaking all the time in the lather. Rinse and allow them to drip until dry. They will be beautifully shiny.

**616. To Rid a Room of Flies.**—A simple way to get rid of flies from a room is to heat a poker and put it on a piece of camphor. This will give off fumes which are most disagreeable to insect pests.

617. **Button Saving Hint.**—Take two pieces of elastic, three inches long and three quarters of an inch wide, double it and sew each piece where the buttons go, leaving the double end one inch above the top of the trousers and on this sew the button. As the wearer bends over his work the elastic gives and the saving is obvious.

618. **Tea Leaves.**—Do not throw away tea leaves. Collect a week's leaves in a pail. Then pour over one quart of boiling water and leave for one hour. Strain and bottle the brew liquid. This is a splendid gloss-maker if used with a soft piece of flannel on mirrors, glasses or windows, it makes them shine like crystal. It is also the very best cleaner for varnished wood, doors and furniture. Use it also for linoleum.

619. **Plates that are Over-heated** often become badly stained and the brown marks are not easy to remove. To take these marks away, use a cork, and some salt, scatter the salt over the burnt part, and rub it briskly with the cork, a little moisture will help the process, but the salt should not be made too wet.

620. **When Beating Eggs.**—Few housewives know that the addition of a little water to eggs that are to be beaten up for cake-making, or omelettes, will make them beat up more lightly and with a minimum of labour.

621. **Salt—its Many Uses :—**

Salt has many uses perhaps not generally known :—

A gargle of salt and water is often efficacious.

A pinch of salt on the tongue, followed ten minutes after by a drink of cold water, often cures a sick headache.

Salt hardens the gums, makes the teeth white and sweetens the breath.

Salt added to the water in which cut flowers stand keeps them fresh.

Salt used dry in the same manner as snuff will do much to relieve colds, hay-fever, etc.

Salt in warm water, if used for bathing tired eyes will be found very refreshing.

Salt and water will stop hemorrhage from tooth extraction.

A little salt on a damp cloth quickly removes the brown stain on egg-spoons.

When eggs crack, sprinkle a teaspoonful of salt in the water, and the whites will not come through.

Soak brooms in strong salt and water before using and they will last much longer.

Soak your feet in salt and water after dancing and you will feel none of the troubles attendant on tired feet the day after the ball.

New potatoes will scrape much easier if a little salt is dissolved in the water.

622. **To Stop Boots Squeaking** make a small hole in the middle of the sole, and then drive in a piece of a match stick.

623. **To tell Linen from Cotton** wet the tip of the finger and apply it to the material. If linen, the moisture will appear on the other side instantly. If cotton, it will take some time before showing.

624. **Washing Hint.**—Before starting to boil the soiled clothes the preservene way, take all the small articles such as collars, cuffs, lace doyleys, etc., and thread with a bodkin on a piece of tape and tie loosely. This plan saves much time, as the small articles can all be taken out together for rinsing, starching, and can be hung in the same manner for drying.

625. **Peeling New Potatoes.**—When preparing new potatoes for cooking, put them in a pail, just cover with water, and stir vigorously with a stout stick. This removes the peel quickly, and the hands are not stained by scraping.

626. **Loose Cover Hint.**—Loose covers on chairs, sofas, etc., always get so soiled on the elbows where the hands rest. When making the covers, make a square just to fit the soiled part, this can be temporarily fixed with press studs, taken off when soiled, washed and placed on again. This plan saves the washing of the whole cover which is usually not soiled.

627. **When Making a Suet Crust,** either for a suet, meat or fruit pudding, soak a piece of stale bread in water, then before using squeeze out all the moisture possible, then add the soaked bread to the suet and flour. This makes the pudding lighter, also it is a good way of using stale bread.

628. **A Cake Hint.**—When eggs are scarce, to get a rich looking appearance for cakes, etc., use a few drops of butter colouring. This is used by dairy farmers for colouring the butter. A bottle costing about 6d. can be procured at the chemist's, and will last an ordinary household many months. It is perfectly harmless.

629. **To Whiten Glazed Sinks. Scullery Sinks** which have been badly neglected and from which stains cannot be removed by the usual friction powders, can be freed from discolouration by a solution of salts of lemon. Wash the sink to remove all grease with hot soapy water, rinse, and put about two or three tablespoonfuls of the solution into the sink, brushing it in with an old nail brush. When the discolouration has disappeared, remove all trace of the acid by thorough rinsing. Salts of lemon, being a poison should be kept under lock and key.

630. **Coffee Pots.**—Metal coffee pots should always be bright on the inside to insure good coffee. An occasional boiling of soapy water in which a little washing soda is dissolved removes the discolouration. Thorough rinsing afterwards is essential.

631. **A Curtain Hint.**—If curtains, etc., are allowed to dry thoroughly before being starched, they will last clean quite a month longer.

632. **A Pudding Hint.**—When making a roly-poly pudding I always sprinkle a cupful of sifted breadcrumbs on the paste before spreading the jam or treacle. This takes up the jam and prevents it running out of roll when cooking.

633. **To Give Potatoes a Good Colour.**—One teaspoon of vinegar in the water just before the cooking is finished. This prevents old potatoes going black. It makes a great improvement.

634. **Poached Eggs.**—When poaching eggs add little vinegar to water, this prevents the eggs breaking.

635. **To Wash Dirty Handkerchiefs.**—Place the soiled handkerchiefs in a clean bucket. Cover with water. Shred some preservene soap and add a tablespoonful of salt. Place on the fire or gas and bring slowly to the boil. Put them at the back of the range for about an hour. Rinse out in cold water and a squeeze of blue. This saves rubbing which is so disagreeable, when washing such handkerchiefs.

636. **A Table Hint.**—Take an old piece of felt or worn out carpet. Cut into discs and glue one side. Fix on to the legs of tables and chairs. This prevents linoleum from being scratched and also stops the irritating noise when these articles are moved.

637. **Cheap Floor Stain.**—Take an ounce and a half of permanganate of potash crystals. Dissolve in one gallon of boiling water. Stir occasionally to keep colour even. Apply to floor evenly. If colour is desired deeper give second coat. When dry rub over with linseed oil. Costs about 3d. per gallon.

638. **To Remove Smell of Onions, Fish, etc., from Knives.** Knives that smell of onion, fish, etc., should be stuck in a pot of earth for a time and all smell will disappear.

639. **To Dust Couches, Cushions, etc.**—To get the dust out of couches, chairs, cushions, mattresses, etc., make some warm water just cloudy with preservene soap, wring out a cloth or old turkish towel, " the larger the better," place on the article to be cleaned, then beat well with a stick or carpet beater and you will be surprised at the result This also prevents the dust from flying about the room.

640. **A Jumper Hint.**—Never peg jumpers, etc., on to the line to dry, but run a cane or broom handle through from cuff to cuff, and suspend to line thus. They will then always keep their shape.

641. **To Clean Outside Steps.**—In winter do not use hearthstone for outside steps, but clean them once thoroughly with pumice-stone. They will then keep clean for weeks, and only require an occasional sweeping.

642. **To Avoid Steam on Windows.**—In winter, when windows are apt to become steamy, rub over once a week with a little methylated spirit. This will prevent them steaming.

643. **A Handy Bootscraper.**—An old bucket, sunk a foot deep in the ground near the back door, makes an excellent bootscraper. In time it will become full, when it can be lifted by the handle, emptied, and replaced.

644. **To Polish Tinware.**—The best way to polish tinware :—wipe over with hot soda and water, then polish with a slice of raw onion.

645. **To Prevent Wooden Tubs from Shrinking.**—Wooden tubs, unless constantly holding water, are liable to shrink. To prevent this, paint over the outside with glycerine.

646. **To Restore the Colours of a Faded Carpet.**—First beat and sweep it, then rub it over with warm water and turpentine.

647. **An Old Broom Hint.**—When an old broom or brush has seen its best days, burn off any remaining bristles and then bind over, where the bristles were, with old flannel or velvet. Result, an excellent floor polisher.

648. **An Improvement on the Perambulator.**—The handle should be made to slip in and out so that it could be fixed on either end, not a fixture, one end only as it is now. By being made to take out and fit in the reverse end when very windy, during the winter many a child would escape a cold as the pram could be reversed by only changing the handle. All prams should have handles to fix on either end. Of course a handle could be fixed both ends, but how unsightly.

649. **To Restore Brooms.**—Brooms that have been stood up on the wrong end get crushed. The best way to restore them is as follows :—Put a half-filled kettle on the fire and when the steam comes strongly from the spout apply the crushed part to it. In a minute or so the bristles will rise to their original position. While steaming, rub the hand briskly over the surface of the broom. Effective for fibre or bristles.

650. **The Morning Shave.**—A good idea is to fill a thermos flask with boiling water each night, it is quite hot for shaving next morning.

**651. Handy Measures :—**

| | | |
|---|---|---|
| 2 teaspoonfuls | equal to | 1 desertspoonful. |
| 2 desertspoonfuls | ,, | 1 tablespoonful. |
| 6 tablespoonfuls | ,, | 1 teacupful. |
| 1 teacupful | ,, | 1 gill. |
| 1 breakfastcupful | ,, | ½ pint. |
| 1 oz. of Dry Substance | ,, | 1 tablespoonful. |
| 1 oz. of butter | ,, | 1 desertspoonful. |
| ½ lb. flour | ,, | 1 breakfastcupful. |
| 1 pint of flour | ,, | 1 lb. |
| 2 tablespoonfuls water | ,, | ½ gill. |
| 2 tablespoonfuls of solids | ,, | 1 gill. |

1 saltspoonful of salt is a good measure of salt for all puddings.

1 cupful of milk is used for mixing one lb. of flour.

1 oz. is equal to three penny pieces ; ½ oz. three half pennies ; ¼ oz. one threepenny and one half-penny.

**652. A Knife Sharpener.**—Get a roll of half-inch adhesive tape and cut off a long strip to go round the hand wheel. Press this to the metal rim of the wheel until it adheres firmly. Next cut a strip of fine emery cloth and glue to the tape on the wheel, wind a strip of cotton cloth, or similar thing, round the emery to hold it in place until the glue is dry. After twenty-four hours the wheel is ready for sharpening knives, scissors and pencils. This does not prevent the machine being used in the ordinary way. When the emery strip is worn out, another may be put in its place.

**653. When a Rug or Carpet curls up at the Corners,** a useful carpet fastener is available which takes the form of a snap fastener. The stud is fixed on to a small screw which is easily screwed into the floor, and the eyelet is sewn on the underside of the carpet or rug. They are obtainable in two sizes to suit a light or heavy carpet, and make the laying down or lifting of a carpet a matter of a few moments.

654. **To Test Water.**—The simplest way to do it is to draw a tumblerful at night, put a lump of sugar into it and leave the glass in a warm room. If the water next morning is clear, then it is quite pure, but if it should appear cloudy or milky it is unfit for drinking.

655. **A Rug for Push Cart.**—To keep baby warm and comfortable out-of-doors. Instead of a rug or shawl for the child's legs when sitting in a push cart, make a pillow case shape rug of blanket cloth or any warm material. Braid or pipe edges with ribbon or braid and embroider if liked. Sew two strong tapes on to the open end and tie to the back of a push-cart. The child's legs are tucked safely inside the pillow case which comes up snugly to about the child's waist. There can be a lining for extra warmth.

656. **Ideal Containers for Pantry.**—Keep dry goods, coffee, rice, ground rice, etc., in Horlick's milk bottles. They are air-tight, need no labels, and when wiped with a damp cloth shine and look very clean in a cupboard or on a shelf. The large size are very useful for bottling fruit or keeping biscuits or buns, and, moreover, you can count them easily.

657. **For a Cheap, Economical and Powerful Disinfectant buy Sheep Dip from the Chemist.**—If in a block, break off a small piece, scald it and when cold put in a bottle, using a little for sinks and lavatories. Put a very little in the water to wash tiles, or stone floors ; it fetches the dirt off and is not harmful to the hands.

658. **When Scrubbing Floors, Boards or Flags,** I always rub the soap on first, dry. This way saves the soap and I find the scrubbing not nearly so hard. It is the rinsing that requires the effort. If white boards are washed and scrubbed in cold water in this manner the result will be very pleasing after a few times.

659. **Black-leading Hint.**—To save time and labour in blackleading, moisten the blacklead with ammonia, the most brilliant and lasting polish will be the result. The grate never looks grey after it has been done this way, and it will last for weeks with an occasional brushing up.

660. **To Prevent Door from Banging.**—Make a weight of any small thing, heavy enough to keep the door open. A half brick or an old iron weight will do. Cover it neatly with carpet or other thick, soft material to make it noiseless. Attach to it a length of strong cord. Put the weight on the floor beside the door. Slip the cord under the door, draw it tightly and tie it firmly to the door handle on the opposite side from the weight. It is always in place, slips noiselessly along the floor, keeps the door at any angle.

661. **When Visiting a Sick Friend.**—Never enter a sick room if you are in a perspiration, for the moment your body cools it is in a state likely to absorb the infection and give you the disease ; nor visit the sick room with an empty stomach as this disposes the system more readily to receive the contagion. In attending a sick person, place yourself where the air passes from door to window to the bed of the diseased person or the fire place, as the fire draws the infectious vapour in that direction, and you would run much danger from breathing it.

662. **To Preserve Lemons.**—Put a layer of sand an inch deep in an earthenware pan. Place lemons not touching each other stalk downwards ; on this, cover with sand

and then put other layers in same way till the pan is full. The sand should be perfectly dry. They will then keep for months if stored in a cool place.

663. **A Wringer Hint.**—If your wringing machine is running very hard, just try throwing a pailful of boiling suds over the wheel parts and turn quickly, and you will find this is much better than oiling and is less trouble.

664. **The Door Mat.**—Place a double thickness of brown paper under it to collect the dust for easy removal.

665. **To Mend Broken Glass.**—Melt a little isinglass in spirits of wine and add a small quantity of water. Warm the mixture gently over a moderate heat. When the isinglass has thoroughly melted, the mixture will form a transparent glue, which will stick glass firmly, and scarcely be noticed.

666. **To Soften Water.**—The hardest water can be softened and much labour saved on washing day by mixing 2 teaspoonfuls of glycerine in a tumbler of water. Use a little as required in the washing water.

667. **Cleaning Water Bottles.**—Crush the shell of an egg small enough to go through neck of bottle, add warm water and shake well. Result :—a clean and nicely polished glass.

668. **Medicine Clock.**—A small clock beyond repair can be used in a sick room. Set the hands when next dose of medicine is due. This relieves the memory.

669. **Substitute for Casserole.**—A common marmalade or jam jar. Food cooks perfectly with no attention. Easy to dish up and food retains all nutriment. Cut up meat, etc., cover with very little water, with greased paper at top.

670.  **Mending Stockings.**—If a piece of net is tacked over the hole on the wrong side before darning, and then darned on the right side the repair will hardly be seen. This method requires less wool, takes less time and is much stronger.

671.  **Cleaning Straw Hats.**—A small quantity of peroxide of hydrogen rubbed well into the hat with an old tooth brush, and well rinsed, will be whiter than if salts of lemon, or oxalic acid, be used.

672.  **Restoring Pearl Buttons.**—To restore pearl buttons to their original lustre, rub with a little olive oil and preservene soap, then sprinkle with nail powder and polish well with a chamois leather.

673.  **Mint, Parsley and all Herbs** remain fresh much longer if placed in a basin covered with saucer so as to make it air-tight, than if placed in water where they soon become decomposed and unfit for food.

674.  **A Cooking Hint.**—If apples and blackberries are first cooked separately and then mixed when cooked it will be found that the apples are quite tender.  If cooked together the acid of the berries acts on apples making them leathery, and no amount of cooking will alter.

675.  **To Clean a Beaver Collar.**—Rub some clean hot bran into the collar till all dirt is removed.  Shake out bran and wrap collar in blue tissue paper into which is sprinkled powdered magnesia.  Leave a day or two, then shake well and collar will be quite clean.

676.  **To Prevent Damp Beds.**—The best way to prevent a bed from becoming damp if left for a week or two, is to leave a blanket on the top of the bed after it is made. Take the blanket off before using and you will then find the bed quite safe.

677. **Uses of Lemons.**—Lemons have many uses besides those of flavouring. If you have a throbbing headache, slice a lemon and rub the pieces over the brow, and the pain will soon go way. If your hair is falling out, rub slices of lemon thoroughly over the scalp and into the roots, washing the head afterwards with warm soft water. A cup of tea is improved with slices of lemon in place of milk. Pure lemon juice will rout giddiness and sea-sickness. If you have a wart or vexatious corn rub lemon juice into it, and in time it will disappear. Bid defiance to mosquitoes with a touch of lemon juice. To improve the appearance of the hands, mix lemon juice and glycerine ; rub your hands with this at night and wear large old gloves till morning.

678. **Sewing Hints.**—When making button-holes in fine soft material, lay a piece of lining or calico under the buttonhole spaces. Stitch each side the length the button-hole is to be, with the sewing machine or firmly by hand, and cut between stitching. Buttonholes are always best worked with silk. Cut lining away after working.

679. **Wire Mattresses.**—These are quickly cleaned by using a bicycle pump, also if a lighted candle is run along the rolled wire edges it soon burns up the fluff which gathers there.

680. **Pillow Ticks.**—After washing and drying pillow ticks rub the inside well with preservene soap slightly damped. This will prevent the feathers or horsehair working through and also keeps out moths.

681. **Short Bead Curtains.**—The materials required are cream macramé twine and large glass beads. For curtains twelve inches in depth, cut the twine into lengths of about thirty-two inches. Take one piece and mark the centre with a pin. Make an ordinary loop knot at each side and as near the centre as possible. Thread a bead and make a

knot one and a half to two inches below the central knots, so that the bead is kept in this position. Thread more beads at fairly uniform distances until there are about four inches left. Then thread six beads together and make a double knot at the end to prevent them from slipping off. Complete sufficient strings to stretch across the window. Take a ball of twine and form one chain. Then connect the strands of beads by joining each loop into a chain with one chain between. The loops are for the insertion of a brass rod. Finish off the top by a row of trebles into each chain.

682. **Useful Mops.**—You can make useful mops from old stockings. Cut them into pieces six inches long and two inches wide. Press a small round of leather on to a large screw, then press each length of stocking through the middle. Continue until screw is full. Screw mop head on to broom stick.

683. **Labour Saving Clothes Line.**—The following arrangement will be found very useful in damp weather where the clothes line extends over the garden or lawn. Procure two small pulleys, attach one to the clothes post and the other to the wall of the house. Reeve the clothes line through these pulleys and securely fasten the two ends making a double line. It will now be possible to stand near the house. Peg the clothes on to one line and, as each piece is fixed, a pull on the other line will send it out over the garden.

684. **The Easiest Way to Empty a Feather Bed.** Open the tick at one end for about one foot. Stitch the clean tick to the dirty one and work the feathers through This prevents the feathers flying.

685. **Venetian Blind Cords.**—To renew Venetian Blind cords without removing the blinds pull the blind to the top and cut the cord where it is thin, whilst someone holds the

blind.   Join the new piece of cord to the old, just drawing
them together with thread so that they meet ; but do not
overlap.   Gently lower the blind, and pull the old cord
through from the bottom until the new cord appears.
Cut away old cord and tie a knot in new.

686.  **Laying Linoleum.**—Never lay linoleum when it is
cold but leave it at least for twenty-four hours in a warm
room so that the heat may penetrate thoroughly to the
centre of the roll or it will crack and peel when it is unrolled.
The floor should be scrubbed, and before it is entirely dry
the linoleum should be unrolled slowly and carefully,
then cut and laid in place.   The slight dampness will not
injure the linoleum but will cause it to stretch.   In a
few days it can be tacked down, no wrinkles then appearing,
as would otherwise be the result.   At least once a year
the linoleum should be varnished.

687.  To prevent **Venetian Blind-tapes** from shrinking
after washing, tack them on to the top of the blinds while
wet.   Put the laths in and let them dry.   The weight of
the laths prevents shrinkage.

688.  **An Excellent Bed-warmer** can be made with
cherry stones.   Make a good strong flannel bag.   Partially
fill it with washed and dried cherry stones.   Put the stones
into a hot oven for a few minutes, then turn them into the
bag and tie up.   These will keep hot all night and last for
years.   They are greatly used in Switzerland.

689.  **Washing Poultry, etc.**—White or light plumaged
poultry, pigeons, canaries, etc., for exhibition or sale must
be washed.   Ordinary yellow or coloured soaps are always
liable to leave discoloured feathers.   Well lather in a tub
of fairly warm water into which shavings of preservene
soap have been dissolved, to remove the dirt, scrubbing the
feet and gently washing the comb and lobes.   Rinse in
clean water and again wash in a fresh bath of lather, to

which has been added the slightest " dip " of the " blue bag "—working with a little pressure of the hand " feather ways." Rinse in plain warm water to remove all the suds— working the way of the feather. Dry with clean towel, and place in a clean basket near a " slow " fire, or in warm room for twelve hours for bird to " plume " itself.

690. **To Wash a Feather Boa.** Make a good lather with tepid water and preservene soap. Place the boa in this and pull and squeeze it through the hands until all the dirt is extracted. Rinse it in clean tepid water, and run the boa through a wringer if possible. Place it in a towel and squeeze as dry as possible. Then stand near a fire and shake the boa until quite dry. This will make it fluffy.

691. **Home-made Stair Rods.**—Procure the number required of ordinary school canes, and cut them into even lengths. Cut off the loose fibres, and paint over with good gold paint. When placed in the rod brackets over the carpets they will be indistinguishable from the very best brass ones.

692. **To Dog Lovers.**—To produce a beautiful gloss on a dog's coat, and to free its body entirely of all vermin wash the dog in tepid water well rubbing its coat with preservene soap. Rub briskly with the hands to produce a good lather, rinse and put two ounces of salts of tartar into the bath, wash again with a good lather and rub thoroughly, especially under the neck and body, again rinse with tepid water. Dry with a hot, coarse towel, and the skin will be beautifully clean and no trace whatever of vermin will be seen on the animal. Use less salts of tartar for a small dog.

693. **To Skin Tomatoes.**—Tomatoes may be easily skinned by immersing them for a few minutes in hot water.

694. **A Spray for Garden Insects.**—A solution of preservene soap to which a little paraffin has been added is a good method of ridding a garden of insects. Mix well by using the garden syringe and afterwards spray plants, etc.

695. **To Cut Onions.**— Cut the onion in halves. Cut nearly through from top to bottom several times and then from side to side. Then cut right through from top to bottom and the onion is chopped ready for use.

696. **Burns.**—A simple yet complete cure for burns is to apply as a poultice equal quantities of shredded soap and raw potato. For very slight burns a smear of soap is very soothing and effective as it prevents air getting to the burnt part.

697. **For Chilblains.**—Put the hands or feet into salt and hot water as hot as can be borne. Soak about twenty minutes. Repeat if not better. This is only recommended when the skin has not broken.

698. **For Warts.**—Wet them and rub a little common house soda on. Do this each day for about ten days.

699. **To Prevent Moth.**—A bar of preservene soap cut into small squares about one or one and a half inches. Place in drawers and boxes. This is a splendid preventative for moths and spiders.

700. **Fruit Picking.**—Nail an ordinary half-pound coffee tin (with a sharp edge) on the end of a bamboo flag pole. When this is put under the fruit, it snaps off and drops into the tin without injury.

701. **To Wind Wool,** turn a chair upside down on another chair and put the wool round the four legs. This will save the trouble of another person holding it for you.

702. **Sleeping Bag for Baby.**—Baby may be allowed to sleep comfortably in his pram during the day if he is slipped into a sleeping bag made from old blankets. Hooks and eyes fasten these bags on the shoulders when the little one has been tucked inside.

703. **Hints on Fruit Preserving.** (1) Always buy fresh dry fruit. It is false economy to use damaged fruit. (2) Use the best lump sugar. (3) A brass preserving pan is the best to use. A small piece of butter with the fruit, prevents it sticking, lessens the scum, and gives the jam a shiny appearance. (4) Never put the sugar in until the fruit has boiled half-an-hour. It is the fruit which requires cooking—not the sugar. If the sugar is boiled the same length of time as the fruit, the jam will be a dark colour. (5) Always put the jam into hot jars, and fasten down immediately. (6) Store in a dry, cool place.

704. **When Clothes Catch Fire.**—It cannot be emphasised too often that " calmness and promptitude " are the watchwords in case of clothing on fire. The effective treatment to be followed is simple in the extreme, but the question of safety or the reverse is usually a matter of seconds. Do not therefore leave the room to seek for help ; it is better to make some attempt to relieve the victim yourself. To stop the progress of the fire, the supply of air must be cut off from the flames. To do this, induce the person to lie flat down on the floor, to prevent the flames spreading or reaching the head. Throw the heaviest available rug or garments over the head, and round the burning clothing and at the same time roll the person on the ground. A determined rush and instant action will work wonders. If one's own clothing catches fire when alone in a room, the same treatment applies. Seize the nearest thing to fling round the burning clothing, and above

all do not run to call for help, for the flames will quickly envelop the whole body. If there is absolutely nothing to wrap round the flames, roll on the floor.

705. **How to Tie a Shoe Lace.**—Proceed exactly as if you were tying an ordinary bow, but before drawing it up, pass the right hand loop through the knot, and give a steady pull on both loops. In untying, be sure to pull the right-hand string, and you will have no trouble.

706. **To Get Rid of Rats.**—Place a large stone at the bottom of a barrel, add sufficient water to allow stone to show above enough for the rat to stand on. Cover the head of the barrel with stiff brown paper, sprinkled with cheese for the first night. The following night cut paper in form of a cross, and add more cheese. The first rat falling in will get on the stone. His cries will soon attract the others, who will follow, and quickly drown.

707. **To Mend Clothes Invisibly.**—Carefully smooth the frayed portion round the tear, and place a small piece of material moistened with thin gum under the hole. Place a heavy weight on top, and when dry it is only possible to find the hole by careful search.

708. **To Clean Photographs.**—Cotton wool dipped in methylated spirit will clean a photograph without injuring the surface.

709. **To Restore a Brown Leather Bag.**—Scrub the bag well with a nailbrush dipped in milk, and rubbed on a piece of preservene soap. Dry well and polish with brown boot polish. Rub hard with a clean rag.

710. **Home-made Down Quilt.**—Fold the old one in four and stitch the corners. Take a large piece of cotton wool and put one piece on either side. Stitch at the corners to keep in place. Cover with a cretonne or sateen cover.

711. **Cleaning White Linen Blinds.**—Lay the blind flat on a kitchen table and sprinkle over a mixture of equal parts of salt and bath brick. Scrub with a stiff dry laundry brush. Shake well and repeat the process on the other side of the blind. The very dirty parts may require a second treatment.

712. **To Sweeten Rancid Butter.**—Melt and skim the butter. Put into the fat a piece of toast free from burn. In a few minutes the butter will lose its offensive taste and smell and can be left to get firm again.

713. **To Make Burning Oil** for a bicycle lamp. Place a small piece of lard in paraffin oil ; this will give a bright, smokeless light.

714. **Clothes Line should be kept clean.**—Wind the clothes line evenly round a board (such as the mangle board) moisten with warm water and rub well with pre-sevene soap. Leave for half an hour. Then scrub well with a stiff brush. Rinse well, and stretch between the line posts as on wash day. Leave till thoroughly dry.

715. **Home-made Tapers.**—Melt candle ends in a saucer and draw some short lengths of string through the warm wax. When set you have some home-made tapers.

716. **Charcoal for the Larder.**—A saucer of charcoal in the larder will prevent the odours of certain foods from tainting other food, especially butter and milk. Meat, fish and poultry can be kept fresh in hot weather by being sprinkled with a little powdered charcoal. This washes away easily just before cooking.

717. **Before Mangling Clothes** rub mangling rollers with a cloth rubbed over with preservene soap. This puts a finishing gloss on the clothes, table-cloths, napkins, etc., and saves ironing.

718. **To Ease a Boot or Shoe.**—If a boot or shoe pinches in any particular part, a cloth wrung out in very hot water and laid over the place while the boot is on the foot, will expand the leather and give relief.

719. **To Prevent Hooks and Eyes Rusting** boil them in strong soda water before using and they will not rust when washed later.

720. **To Preserve Parsley.**—Wash freshly gathered parsley, and put it into slightly boiling water. Boil for three minutes. Take out and drain. Lay on a sieve in front of the fire and dry as quickly as possible. Store in bottles in a dry place. When required, place in a dish of warm water for five minutes.

721. **New Life for Ferns.**—If ferns are not doing well try giving them a few drops of castor oil at the roots and setting them in a pail of water all night. In a weeks time, they will be putting out new shoots. This must not be done oftener than every two or three months.

722. **To Separate Two Tumblers.**—When two tumblers become fixed inside each other, it is often a difficult matter to separate them. Pour cold water into the inner glass and then stand the outer one in rather warm water. As a result of this the inner glass contracts and the outer one expands, so that the two are easily separated.

723. **Destroying Blackbeetles.**—To rid a kitchen of black beetles a little strong essence of peppermint should be poured down the crevices or holes in the floor and covered in with putty. The putty must be used while it is fresh.

724. **Airtight Corks.**—When bottling fruit or vegetables it is absolutely essential that the corks are air-tight. To ensure this dip the corks in a mixture of mutton suet and white wax. Fix into the bottles and leave to harden.

725. **Quassia.**—Quassia is one of the busy housewife's friends. If two ounces are added to all scrubbing water it will keep vermin away. Quassia chips can be bought from the chemists.

726. **Empty Cotton Reels.**—To make hangers either for doors or cupboards, a good plan is to take empty cotton reels, insert a long screw or nail in each and nail into the place wanted. After which paint or enamel them. Should a room door persist in opening too far back, use one cotton reel, nailing it into position on the floor behind the door.

727. **Mushrooms.** To distinguish mushrooms from poisonous fungi. Sprinkle a little salt on the spongy part or gills of the sample to be tried. If they turn yellow, they are poisonous, if black, they are wholesome. Allow the salt to act before you decide.

728. **Oil Paintings.**—Oil paintings can be cleaned by using a cut potato. Rub over the painting cutting a bit more off the potato as it gets soiled. Then wash with a sponge dipped in cold water and dry.

729. **To remove Iron Scorches.**—When an article becomes scorched in ironing, lay it over a large plate and moisten the scorched part with a jelly-like mixture of soap, starch and water. Lay a piece of glass over all, and place in the sun. Re-moisten until all the stain is removed.

730. **Vacuum Flasks.**—Tea or coffee should not be mixed with milk before placing in a vacuum flask, for the flask will smell of sour milk, however well it is washed. A special flask should be kept for milk, and the cork placed in an airy spot, first washing it in hot water. It should be washed again before being used. After use, the flask itself should first be washed with soapy water, rinsed several times and well drained. Before filling a flask

with hot drink allow a little boiling water to rest in it, and if a cold drink is needed rinse out the flask with cold water. Corks for a vacuum flask need the greatest care, as they absorb the odour of hot beverages. They should be scrubbed and dried at the earliest convenience after the flask has been used.

731. **Skirt and Sleeve Boards.**—An old mantle-board, shaped a little, will make a splendid skirt board. Cover it tightly with a piece of old blanket and finally with white sheeting. There must be no creases at all, or ironing will be very difficult.

732. **To Tighten Scissors.**—Press a red hot poker on each side of the rivet. This will expand the rivet and tighten the scissors.

733. **To Renovate Old Golf Balls.**—Drop each ball separately into a pail of almost boiling water. Lift out when the skin of the ball is softened. Rub the ball smartly between the corrugated sides of two ordinary butter spades. When all the gashes and bruises have been rubbed out, drop the ball into a pail of cold water to harden. Dry, then take a little golf ball paint in the palm of the hand and rub the ball between the palms, till evenly covered. Drop each ball on to a clean newspaper and allow to dry.

734. **Bass Brooms.**—When new, these should be soaked for twenty-four hours in cold water to prevent the fibres breaking. If, during use, this treatment is repeated occasionally the life of the broom is prolonged.

735. **Blunt Needles.**—If a sewing machine needle is blunt, sharpen it on the broken edge of a broken saucer or plate.

736. **The Uses of Vinegar.**—Greasy dishes are more easily washed and metal work can be brightened with half the labour, while rust is a simple matter to remove if vinegar is used. If a few drops are burnt on a hot plate or shovel, a room fouled with the smell of smoke is quickly cleaned, and the odour of cabbage, fish and onions can be cleaned from pans if vinegar is used. Mixed with black-lead it will give an added brilliancy to the grate, and in conjunction with olive oil will improve the polish of furniture.

737. **To Clean Copper.**—Prepare some plate-cleaning powder with three parts liquid ammonia and one part water. Mix well, and apply with a duster, rubbing well. Then polish in the usual way.

738. **A Darning Hint.**—Hold the darning wool for a few minutes over the spout of a kettle of boiling water. This shrinks the wool and when the stockings are washed there is no fear of mended parts shrinking, and so tearing away and making a break round the hole that was first mended.

739. **Hot Water Bottles** or other articles made of india-rubber should be washed every two months with water to which a little soda or ammonia has been added. This will prevent them from perishing and getting hard.

740. **Varnished Walls.**—Tea is an excellent cleanser for varnished papers of any sort. Wash the walls well with a mop in a warm solution of water and tea, and when thoroughly dry, polish over with sweet oil and turpentine.

741. **Cork Mats.**—Save all the corks you can get and when you think you have a sufficient number, buy a piece of fine wire netting the size you want to make your mat. The corks have to be fitted into the holes of the netting. You may have to cut them so that they must be all the

same depth. Use a sharp knife for this. Each should
fit the spaces fairly tightly. When every hole is filled,
the edges of the mat must be bound with leather, which
should be tacked on with brass headed nails.

742. **Coal Scuttle**—to renew bottom. Procure a round,
thick piece of wood, place the scuttle on top of it to get
the right size, then cut the wood half an inch less than the
bottom of scuttle.

743. **When Petersham** gets limp, rub thickly with
soap on the side facing skirt. Then iron with hot iron.

744. **To Clean Alabaster.**—Remove any stains by
sponging with a piece of flannel moistened with spirits of
turpentine and dipped in finely powdered pumice-stone.
Wash with warm soapy water to which has been added
a little borax, then rinse and wipe dry. Polish with a soft
brush dipped in plaster of paris.

745. **To Mend an Enamel Bowl.**—Mix some ordinary
building cement with cold water to the consistency of a
thick cream. Spread evenly over the hole, and leave to
dry for a day or two.

746. **Cheap Night Lights.**—Place a small piece of camphor into a bowl or glass of water so that it will float.
This may be lighted and will not only prove a good night
light but also an excellent disinfectant.

747. **To Tan Rabbit Skins.**—Make some strong soap suds.
Allow to cool, then thoroughly wash the skins and rinse
them. Make a solution of half-a-pound each of alum and
salt in hot water, and put into a tub. When cool, place
the skins in the solution for twelve hours then hang them
out over a pole to dry. Now take one ounce each of
saltpetre and pulverised alum and sprinkle it on the skins.
Rub well in on the flesh side, lay flesh sides together and
hang in shade to dry, turning the under one uppermost

each day until thoroughly dry. Scrape the skins thoroughly and carefully with a blunt knife and rub with pumice stone.

748. **Frying Hint.** When Frying Fat has got slightly burnt drop a raw peeled potato into the pan for a few minutes and then remove it. All trace of burning will have disappeared.

749. **Drawn Thread Work.**—An easy and quick way to draw threads in linen for hemstitching. Make a lather of soap and apply over the fabric. Allow it to dry and the threads will pull out quite easily.

750. **Wasp Sting.**—Rub a slice of common onion on the sting. If in the throat or mouth, chew an onion slowly and swallow. A certain cure.

751. **To Stain Concrete.**—First scrub well with soap and water and let dry. Then stain the same as wood, with any varnish stain. No polishing is necessary afterwards. Merely take the dust up with a damp cloth.

752. **A Rubber Hot-water Bottle** should never be put away flat so that sides rest against each other. A much better plan is to blow hard into the empty bottle, then screw top on quickly. The air in bottle will keep sides apart, and avoid the danger of leaking.

753. **Cake Tins** greased and sprinkled with a mixture of equal parts of flour and fine sugar, saves the trouble of lining with paper and prevents cakes from sticking.

754. **Draught Excluder.**—Fix a rubber roller, near the bottom of doors. Mount on suitable bracket, so that when the door be shut the roller can be pressed down by the foot to the floor and exclude the draught. A catch should be made which will release with the foot and allow the roller to be pulled up by a small spring—just sufficient to clear the floor.

755. **Cleaning a Wool Rug.**—Tack the rug on to a flat-board the same size as the rug. Prepare a pailful of soap suds with shredded preservene soap, adding a teaspoonful of salt and a dessertspoonful of borax. Rub the soap into the rug with your hands, thoroughly soaking and rubbing it alternately. When the rug is clean rinse it with lukewarm water several times. Put rug in the sun, still stretched on the board, and as it dries, keep rubbing it. When almost dry untack and shake rug vigorously. Hang over a line to air. The tacking down prevents shrinkage.

756. **To Clean Fox Furs.**—Have ready a tub half-full of warm water, into which has been shredded half a bar of preservene soap (and if water is very hard) a teaspoonful of borax. It is advisable to remove fasteners from the fur, and tack lining and padding securely together to keep in place before wetting. Then dip fur in and out of water briskly many times, rubbing soiled parts with the hands, well soaped. If very soiled, repeat this with a fresh lather, then rinse in two waters. If a white fur, add little blue to final rinse. Put through the wringer, then shake well and hang out in good breeze to dry.

757. **Winter Drying.**—When drying clothes in winter, if a handful of common salt be added to the rinsing water it keeps the clothes from freezing until dry.

758. **To Make Your Own Blue.**—Get from the chemist two pennyworth of oxalic acid and Prussian blue mixed. Put it into a quart bottle and fill up with water. This will last a long time, as only a very little at a time is needed for blueing clothes. Besides being cheaper than ordinary blue this mixture never makes the articles streaky or cloudy.

759. **To Clean Children's Toy Animals** of white wool. Shred a small quantity of preservene soap into a basin and with boiling water and make into a thick

lather. When cool, rub into coat of animal with a piece of clean linen until free from dirt, taking care not to make it too wet or the toy may lose its shape. Then with fresh linen rag wrung out of clean water take off superfluous soap and leave to thoroughly dry, in open if possible. Brush fur with a wire brush.

760. **Books.**—Black leather bound books can be much improved by mixing two spoonfuls of black ink and one of sweet oil. Apply to binding with a sponge and allow it to dry.

761. **To Make Labels Stick on Tins.**—Brush some Friars Balsam on the tin and leave to dry. Stick adhesive label on and it will not fall off.

762. **When Plants in Pots** show signs of fading, they can be revived by watering with a solution of ammonia and water—about a teaspoonful to three quarts of water.

763. **Fish Line for Hanging Pictures** is excellent, as it is not only strong, but doesn't show much. Pictures hang more evenly this way than when wire is used.

764. **Wash Neglected Gilt Frames** in the water in which onions have been boiled. This greatly improves their appearance.

765. **When Stoning Raisins** pour boiling water over them and leave for a short time. Then squeeze out the seeds at the stem end. This prevents any of the inside from being wasted.

766. **A Simple Filter** can be made from a clean garden flower pot, 8 or 9 inches high. Place a small sponge into hole at bottom. Then place in pot, layer of charcoal 2 inches deep, a layer of sand and 3 inches of clean gravel. Fix this over some vessel and allow water to pass through the layers into pot. Renew material now and again.

767. **To Prevent Rashers of Bacon from Shrinking** during the process of frying, dip them into flour. This prevents the fat from running.

768. **Leather Hand Bags** can be much improved as follows :—Pierce a new laid egg and draw off the white. Apply with a clean brush at once, putting on thickly. Allow a good time to dry. If colour of leather has gone it must be treated with a little paint before white of egg is used.

769. **To Keep Cheese from Moulding.**—After it has been cut, dip a thin muslin cloth in vinegar, wring out and wrap up the cheese in it.

770. **Books bound in canvas or linen** may be restored by wringing a clean duster in hot water, and rubbing the book cover briskly all over. Dry at once with another rubber.

771. **Pin Cushion.** Dry coffee grounds make an excellent filling for pin cushions. Moreover, the pins placed in a cushion so filled will never rust.

772. **Before Manicuring** make a lather of soap in warm water. Soak the finger tips. This will soften the cuticle without harming the skin.

773. **An Alarm Clock** is a remarkable time-saver if used regularly in the kitchen. When putting a cake or pudding into the oven set the alarm to the time it will need attention. A warning sound from the alarm will help when the hour to prepare dinner or supper arrives.

774. **Potato Boiling.**—A few drops of lemon squeezed into the water will make the darkest looking potato boil white.

775. **An Effective Coin Test.**—Take the suspected coin in one hand, another coin in the other. Hold them edge to edge, and forcibly drag one across the other in the same way that cog-wheels grate together. The milled edge of the counterfeit coin will be stripped clean off and the test will leave no doubt whatever as to the genuineness of the coin. Two genuine coins giving a pleasant, hard clicking sound.

776. **Mangling.**—It is a good plan when folding linen for the mangle to make the fold a different way each week and the clothes will not wear so quickly. The constant fold in one way causes the crease to wear thin and necessitates more mending.

777. **Remedy for Leaking Washing Tubs.**—Boil some ordinary stinging nettles (Urtica dioica) in a strong solution of salt. If the resulting liquid is rubbed liberally into the leaky seams of wooden washing tubs it will coagulate rendering them once more watertight.

778. **A Good Use for Twine.**—Keep all the fine twine till you have a ball of it. Then knit on steel needles a piece about a foot square. Coarse twines make splendid " cloths " for cleaning pots and pans. Fine twine makes excellent dish cloths that are easily and thoroughly cleansed.

779. **A Cake Hint.**—When a level cake is required for icing, make a hole in the middle of the raw cake mixture before putting it into the oven. Raise the mixture up round the sides of the tin. Place the cake in a quick oven, and the cake will have a nice flat surface when it is cooked.

780. **The Care of Lamps.**—Always buy the best paraffin. It lasts longer and is cheaper in the end. Give your lamps a thorough clean weekly. This cleaning must include turning out the container. Once a month you will need

to take the lamps to pieces, boil the burners in hot soda water and wash out the containers letting them get quite dry before using again. Strain the oil into the container, either by putting a piece of muslin inside your funnel or a small wad of cotton wool. Always soak the wicks before using them in vinegar for a quarter of an hour. Then let them hang until perfectly dry and they will last longer and give a steadier, brighter light. To make the chimneys absolutely fireproof, before using, put them into a pan of cold water and bring gradually to the boil. Allow them to boil about fifteen minutes afterwards drawing the pan aside to cool gradually. Dry thoroughly and polish off with a large piece of butter muslin if you have no mop.

781. **Chicken Coops** during the hatching season. Preservene soap makes a good disinfectant and coops washed with preservene enables the hen to sit on her eggs in comfort.

782. **One Use for Stale Bread.**—Dry stale pieces of bread in the oven until crisp right through. Then grind in a nut mill (or very small hole in ordinary mincer). The result is dry bread crumbs, which will keep indefinitely and be ready at once when frying rissoles or fish.

783. **To cut up Candied Peel.**—Instead of tediously cutting up candied peel with a knife, rub it on the suet grater. Nice fine, even slices will be the result and much time will be saved.

784. **An Ordinary Tin Funnel** makes a capital device for a ball of string. Draw the end through the funnel and hang the latter on a nail or hook in the kitchen dresser.

785. **When beating eggs** or the whites of eggs, add a tiny pinch of salt. You will be surprised how much better and quicker they whip up.

786. **Hints on the ever useful Sewing Machine.**—If the sewing machine works badly, open it up and see if bits of fluff have collected under the plate. If so, clean them out. If the stitch keeps on slipping, and you have lately put a new needle in, take the needle out and see if you put it in the right way. The flat side of the needle should go against the screw. To clean a sewing machine that is working heavily is to fill your oil-can with paraffin oil and oil the machine in the usual holes. Then put the machine beside the fire, and leave for a couple of hours. You will then find that the oil has worked out, but that it is now black and full of grit. Wipe the machine carefully, and oil with proper machine oil. Paraffin oil or salad oil must never be used for oiling the sewing machine in the ordinary way. Very often a sewing machine makes a much better stitch if sixty cotton is put on the bobbin and fifty cotton on the top of the machine, threaded through the needle. If you are using forty cotton on top, use fifty on the bobbin.

787. **Bed Valance.**—Instead of tying on the bed valance, knock brass-headed nails into the wood along the sides and bottom of the wire mattress. Then make button-holes along the valance to correspond and it buttons on.

788. **Antimacassars.**—Antimacassars are very old-fashioned now, and are simply dust-catchers. If you have any pretty worked ones, turn them into little narrow bolster cushions to tie on the back of a chair as a head-rest.

789. **Distemper that will wash.**—To every pint of fresh lime add a handful of kitchen salt. Mix with cold water till like cream, then tint with dye or permanganate of potash if you like pink, or laundry blue for pale blue. This distemper will wash twice or three times.

790. **Doors facing outwards,** like the front or back doors, soon look shabby. Do not repaint, but rub over with a flannel dipped in paraffin oil, then polish well with a soft, dry duster.

791. **How to Clean Gilt Picture Frames.**—Put enough flowers of sulphur into a pint of hot water to give it a golden tint. Add four bruised onions. Strain, and when the liquid is cold paint the frames, using a soft paint brush.

792. **How to Clean Japanese Tables.**—First rub with a rag dipped in warm vinegar. This cleans, but makes the varnish cloudy. Polish with a rag dipped in paraffin and then with a dry, soft duster made of butter muslin.

793. **Japanned Trays** which have been marked by hot teapots, etc., should be rubbed with a little sweet oil. This should be polished off, and when dry, the tray to be rubbed with flour and a duster.

794. **A Jelly Hint.**—In making a jelly use only a small quantity of nearly boiling water to dissolve the square, the rest of the required quantity can be made up by adding cold water. In this way a saving in heating water is effected and as a result the jelly sets much more quickly.

795. **A Hint on Smoking.**—The air may be sweetened and cleared of stale smoke smell in a minute. Sprinkle some dried coffee grounds into a shovel of red hot cinders or leave a pail of water in the room before shutting it up for the night.

796. **To Keep Apples for Winter Use.**—Put the apples into casks or bins in layers well covered with dry sand. Each layer should be covered. This preserves them from air, from moisture, and from frost.

797. **A Good and Quick Way to Clean Ivory.**—Make a paste of sal volatile and olive oil. Rub it on with a wash-leather. Leave it to dry in the sun. Brush off and polish.

798. **For Aching Feet.**—Place two tablespoonfuls of paraffin oil in a foot bath and wash feet in the ordinary way with plenty of soap; the slight odour quickly disappears and the relief and comfort is lasting. The paraffin oil gives a fresh, soothing feeling, not obtainable by using salt, etc.

799. **To Cook Old Fowls.**—Instead of steaming, boil for three hours and roast one hour and you will not tell them from chicken.

800. **To Clean a Thermos Flask.**—Put some crushed egg-shells in the bottom of the flask with a little vinegar. Shake well, then half-fill with water and let it stand for a time. Shake again, empty, then rinse thoroughly. Invert the flask in a jug and when dry put away, but do not replace the cork, as this is apt to make the flask musty.

801. **A Waterproof Clothes Line.**—Dissolve a pound of preservene soap in about a gallon of warm water. When completely dissolved, put the clothes line in the mixture and leave half an hour. Now in the same quantity of water, put a pound of alum. Remove the line from the soap water and place it in the alum water. Leave it for an hour and when you remove it you will find the rope absolutely waterproof.

802. **To prevent Milk burning** when scalding, place the milk in a jug inside a saucepan of water and bring to the boil.

803. **To Cure Chilblains.**—Paint them with Friar's Balsam on going to bed, as a rule one application cures, if not, give a second. Not for broken chilblains. Cost 2d. and a 1d. brush, or failing a brush tie a piece of wadding to a match stick and paint with that. A most easy and reliable remedy.

804. **Water Stains on Satin.**—Rub gently with tissue paper in a circular motion. In a few minutes the marks will disappear.

805. **To Clean Patty Pans.**—Put Patty pans into an iron or enamel saucepan with a little dissolved preservene. Boil for about three-quarters of an hour. Remove and dry well with a clean towel and your patty pans will be bright and shining.

806. **Re-proofing a Waterproof Motor Coat.**—Well rub beeswax into the inside of the coat, paying special attention to the seams and places where creases occur. When the material is well covered with wax, iron with a hot iron until the wax thoroughly soaks into the material. The coat will be then found quite waterproof.

807. **Dried Peas or Beans** can be made tender without previous soaking. If brought to the boil and then allowed to stand on the side of the stove for one hour. Re-boil and cook in the usual way. The flavour can be greatly improved if a carrot and an onion with a clove stuck in are cooked with the peas or beans.

808. **To make sure that Tinned Fruit is non-poisonous.** Turn contents into a basin leaving about three table-spoonfuls of syrup or gravy in the tin. Put a sixpence into the tin and let it come to the boil for about three minutes. Remove from the stove, take out the sixpence and if it turns black the food is not fit for use.

809. **Fireproof Glue.** Mix 4 ozs. linseed oil with a hand ful of quicklime. Boil until fairly thick. Spread on tins to cool out of sun, when it will become very hard. This successfully resists fire, and may be easily dissolved and used as ordinary glue.

810. **To Free Windows From Frost.**—Apply a little glycerine with a dry duster and a brilliant polish will result. This is also an excellent remedy for preventing windows steaming if rubbed on inside of glass after the windows are cleaned.

811. **Cloth Cleaning Ball.** Splendid for freshening clothes, particularly of light colour. Mix thoroughly 5 ozs. pipe clay and 1 oz. pulverized French chalk, add 2 ozs. spirits of wine to form a paste, and roll it into a ball. Damp the material with warm water, rub the ball well in, leave for several hours and brush off.

812. **Poisons for Insects.**—Paraffin is very good for exterminating insects of all kinds, especially those which infest furniture, etc. Ants—(1) Use carbolic acid, tobacco water, or a strong solution of spirits of wine and water. Pour into the holes for several days running and persist until the insects are destroyed. Bugs—(1) Make a paste of 1d. alum and boiling water and apply to all infected parts. (2) Fill up crevices with equal parts of flour and alum. (3) Apply camphor or damp articles, such as the woodwork of beds, with spirits of naphtha. Black Beetles—Sprinkle a mixture of borax and powdered lump sugar every night for a week or ten days. Crickets—Sprinkle quicklime near their haunts. Fleas—Oil of pennyroyal is a quick riddance. Lice—Wash body and cloths with a strong solution of pearl-ash and use carbolic soap. Moths— Sprinkle the inside of chests of drawers and cupboards periodically with spirits of turpentine. Wrap furs in naphthalene and newspapers, and keep in airtight boxes.

813. **To Waterproof Tweed at Home.**—Tweed garments may be rendered waterproof and impervious to the heaviest rains if treated as follows :—Into a pail of soft or rain water put ½ lb. sugar of lead and the same quantity of powdered alum. Stir every now and then until mixture

becomes quite clear. Pour it off into another vessel and place the garments therein for twenty-four hours. Hang up to dry without wringing and any coat immersed in this solution is to be recommended in place of a waterproof or raincoat.

814. **To Prevent Water Tasting of Smoke** when boiled on the fire, allow a small piece of wood similar to a match stick to float on top of the water.

815. **When an egg is found to be insufficiently cooked** place a clean darning needle in the centre of the egg. Put back in pot. The egg will set without coming out of the shell.

816. **Milk or Cream that has become sour,** may be sweetened with the aid of a pinch of carbonate of soda. To prevent milk from souring, dissolve half a teaspoonful of California borax in a drop of hot water, mix this with the milk, and it will keep perfectly sweet.

817. **Sweeten Stewed Fruit** after it has been cooked and it will not need half the amount of sugar. When peeling apples, much of the fruit is wasted. If boiling water is poured over the fruit and left a few minutes, the skins can then be removed easily without waste.

818. **For Flannels.**—A teaspoonful of olive oil added to each gallon of water in which flannels are washed, will keep them beautifully soft.

819. **Putty for Rounding Corners.**—Prepare a number of small pellets of putty and after washing out the corners of woodwork in doors, skirtings, mouldings, window-ledges, etc. press one pellet into each corner, round it off neatly and leave to set. When hardened put a dab of paint over the putty to match the rest of the paintwork. Next time paint cleaning has to be done the advantage of not having to poke into corners will be much appreciated.

820. **To Cure Damp Walls.**—Mix 10 ozs. of turpentine, 15 ozs. of chalk, 16 ozs. boiled linseed oil, 5 ozs. resin. Paint the damp wall with this.

821. **To Clean an Ebony Piano.**—A few drops of pure salad oil applied with a warm flannel and polished with a chamois leather will make the case like new.

822. **Home-made Baking Powder.**—6 ozs. bicarbonate soda, 6 ozs. tartaric acid, 2 ozs. ground rice, 1 oz. flour. Press with a rolling pin to crush any lumps and bottle in dry jar.

823. **To Keep Lettuce and Cucumber Fresh.**—If lettuce and cucumber are put on the stone floor and covered with a pudding bowl they will keep fresh for days, much better than being put in water.

824. **Wash Green Vegetables** first in warm water to remove insects. Then rinse in cold water.

825. **A Stamp Hint.**—Postage stamps and gummed labels, that have become stuck together may be separated by being covered with a piece of paper, then pressed with a hot iron. The stamps or labels can then be easily separated and the adhesive will not be damaged.

826. **To Test an Egg.**—Hold it up to the light. If it is fresh, it will be quite clear ; if cloudy it is stale.

827. **To Choose Poultry.** The flesh should be firm and of a pinkish yellow colour. The legs should be pliable and the scales smooth.

828. **China—to Temper—to Prevent Breakages.**—Fill a saucepan with cold water and immerse your gas globes and chimneys in it. Bring it gradually to the boil, afterwards allow it to cool gradually. Valuable china can be treated in this way. This process tempers the china and makes it less liable to crack.

829. **Piano Keys** are liable to get stiff in a damp room. To remove the stiffness rub the sides of the notes with a little blacklead.

830. **Cement for Glass.**—Allow 5 to 10 parts of pure dry gelatine to dissolve in 100 parts of water. To the solution add 10 per cent. of a concentrated solution of bichromate of potash and keep in the dark. When articles joined by this cement are exposed to the light, the gelatine film is acted upon by the chemical rays. The chromate is partially reduced and the film of cement becomes extremely tough and durable.

831. **An Apple Drink.**—Put a tart apple well baked and mashed into a pint of boiling water. Beat well, cool and strain. Add a little sugar. It is a nice cooling drink for an invalid.

832. **Barley Water.**—Two ounces Pearl Barley washed through cold water. Boil for a few minutes in one quart of water, strain off the water, then boil the barley in two quarts of water until it boils down to one quart.

833. **A Trap for Snails.**—Snails are very fond of bran. Spread a little on the ground and cover it with cabbage leaves, they will crawl underneath the leaves, when you will be able to destroy them.

834. **To Make Watchmaker's Oil** which never corrodes or thickens. Take some neatsfoot oil and put some lead shavings into it. Allow these to stand together for a considerable time (the longer the better). This is the watchmaker's oil sold at 18d. a drachm. The universal remedy for clocks, chronometers and watches.

835. **How to Treat a Stye on the Eye.**—If dealt with at once, it may be cut short by bathing the part in a very strong and warm solution of boric acid. But if any

swelling and redness are present, no attempt should be made to arrest the stye. When inflammation occurs materials are poured out into the tissues from the blood vessels. Now, if these materials are allowed to form pus (matter) and this is discharged, the parts resume their healthy state, and there is no sign of anything ever having been amiss. But if the pus is cut short the chances are in favour of a permanent swelling and some redness. This applies to all boils, pimples, etc., wherever situated. One should always help the matter to come to a head and be discharged. Hot fomentations always help.

836. **Violins—to Polish.**—Three parts Neatsfoot oil, one part eau de Cologne. Apply sparingly with soft cloth, afterwards polish with washleather. Especially good for removing resin, grease, etc. from violins.

837. **To Make a Barometer at Home.**—Take a small empty vinegar bottle, and an empty 1 lb. glass jam jar. See that the bottle can sit comfortably upside-down in the jar. Now fill the bottle about half-full of water, coloured with red ink—or any other bright colouring matter. Place the jar up-side-down on top of the bottle and reverse, allowing the water to flow into the jar until only an inch or two of water remains in the neck of the bottle This column of water in the neck will rise for fine weather and drop for rain or fierce wind.

838. **To Filter Water.** Boil and strain through blotting paper folded fan shape to form a funnel.

839. **To Prepare Waterglass.**—For preserving eggs, etc., boil and cool nine quarts of water. When cold add one quart of sodium silicate and mix thoroughly.

840. **To Prevent Cotton from Knotting.** Always thread the loose end through the needle, and knot the end broken off the reel.

841. **To Launder Corduroy**. Fill a bath with warm soapy water. Wash the garment by lifting it up and down in the water. Rinse until all soap is removed. Without wringing or squeezing carry the garment to the line. Shake occasionally while drying. When thoroughly dry, brush to restore the nap.

842. **To Replace Tips on Shoe Laces.**—When a tip pulls off, dip the end of the lace in melted sealing wax, of the same colour and shape to a point with the fingers still warm.

843. **To Run Ribbon in Lingerie Quickly.**—Before removing the ribbon preparatory to washing sew to one end a piece of tape the same length. As the ribbon is drawn out the tape takes its place. The joining is then severed and the garment laundered. Then the ribbon is once more caught with a few stitches to the end of the tape and is drawn into place again as the tape is pulled out.

844. **To Clean Paint Brushes.**—Wash in turpentine, followed by soda water. Rinse in clear water and shape carefully by drawing through the fingers. Never allow brushes to stand on bristles while drying. If to remain unused for some time moisten with linseed oil before putting away.

845. **To Draw Out Splinters.**—Pound finely a small piece of resin. Place this on a piece of linen and drop some hot candle grease on the resin. Apply it to the affected part. The splinter will be drawn out in a very short time.

846. **A Jam Making Hint.**—To make jam or marmalade, look clear without skimming, add a piece of butter the size of a small egg, about quarter of an hour before removing from the fire. The jam will look quite clear and will not stick to the jars when turned out for use.

847.  **A Useful Frying Hint.**—Always put a small piece of bread crust into the pan before frying fish. This prevents the fat from spluttering and shows by its brown colour just when the fat is ready for the fish to be put in.

848.  **Washing Skin Rugs.**—These may be washed with a lather of preservene soap, shredded into hot water. Spread the rug out on a flat surface then scrub, using discretion in the vigour of scrubbing.  Afterwards rinse very thoroughly in clear cold water. The rugs should dry in the open in a good, strong breeze.

849.  **Eliminate the Pudding Cloth.**—Much time can be saved if a piece of greased paper be tied over the pudding instead of the usual linen cloth which requires so much water to clean it.  After tying round with a string make a loop from side to side whereby the basin can be easily lifted from the saucepan.

850.  **Glass Rod for Short Window Curtains.**—Use $\frac{5}{16}$ to $\frac{3}{8}$ in. glass rod, which may be bought and cut the desired length at any chemical laboratory furnishers.  If the ends are rough, a little sandpaper or a fine file, such as an old manicure file, will smooth them.  The curtains slip on and off very easily.  No cleaning, no sagging and always smart.

851.  **To keep your Dishcloths sweet.**—Wash them with preservene soap and a little borax and dry in the open air.

852.  **Alarm Clock** that rings too loudly can be moderated by slipping an elastic band around the bell.  The wider the band the stronger the suppression, and a few experiments will demonstrate just what width is most desirable.

853.  **To make a Lamp Wick.**—A very good lamp wick can be made from an old felt hat, cut in strips.  It is far better than real lamp wick.

854. **How to Discover a Dead Rat.**—To locate a dead rat in a room catch half-a-dozen blue bottle flies and slip them into a glass jar. Let the flies out in the room where you suspect the rat is and sit down whilst they fly round. Within an hour they will have scented the rat and all be buzzing round one spot. That is where your rat is. You can then take up the board and remove the pest.

855. **Egg Substitute.**—One tablespoonful of golden syrup dissolved in half a pint of warm milk equals three eggs.

856. **To Remove Fast Stoppers.**—Place the bottle in a basin with enough hot water to reach to the top of the neck. The air in the bottle as well as the glass will expand and loosen the stopper.

857. **Soaped Thread for Beads.**—Threading beads will not be such a long and tedious business if the thread is first passed a few times over a bar of preservene soap. This gives it a stiffness which makes it pass easily through the tiny holes. At the same time strengthening the thread.

858. **Patent Leather.**—Black patent shoes can be cleansed easily and quickly if petrol is used. Dip a soft rag in petrol, rub it over the shoes and polish with a dry pad.

859. **Rusty Pen Nibs.**—If pens are stuck into a potato when not in use, the nibs will not rust and the pens will always be in good condition.

860. **To Trap Earwigs.**—An easy and quick method is to lay down corrugated strawboard such as is used for packing bottles, &c. The earwigs crawl into the crevices and can then be destroyed, leaving the cupboard or pantry clear.

861. **To Polish Oilcloth.**—Wash with a soft cloth with a little soap in the water ; when dry apply floor polish, and let it remain on four hours. Then polish with clean cloth or mop. This will give a brilliant finish, also last much longer than the usual way of finishing straight away.

862. **To Remove Blood Stains from Linen.**—Well soap the articles and roll up tightly, put in cold water, add a little soda and soak. Rinse in clean water, and put in copper with cold water and soap, bring to boil and boil half an hour.

863. **To Clean Paint off Glass.**—Rub the glass with paraffin, wash off with soap and water, polish with whitening with a soft cloth, and the glass will be bright and clear.

864. **To Clean Greasy Sinkstones.**—Damp the sink and sprinkle over with chloride of lime, let it remain on all night, and wash off with clean water. This will clean off all grease and leave the stone a good colour ; no need for scrubbing.

865. **To Keep the Dust Down.**—When sweeping a room or carpets, sprinkle with tea-leaves squeezed from the teapot. This will prevent the dust from rising and save time and trouble of covering the furniture over.

866. **To Kill Moths in Furniture.** Sprinkle powdered alum freely under carpets, and in the crevices of upholstered chairs, settees, etc.

867. **Socks for boots** can be made from an old felt hat.

868. **When a Saucepan Boils Dry and Burns** it can be saved by putting a piece of butter the size of a walnut in the pan, allow it to melt, then pour in hot water. If it has been under the steamer it can be used at once.

869. **Never Throw Away Preservene Soapsuds.**—When the washing is done they are the finest thing for cleaning paint, and in fact for all cleaning. To clean a tiled hall or kitchen floor, scrub well with the soapsuds. When dry, polish with floor polish. This can now be kept clean with a mop and saves continual washing.

870. **Instead of Troubling to Make Starch** for large tablecloths, tray-cloths, etc., add one tablespoonful of methylated spirits to the last rinsing water. This stiffens them sufficiently; they are easier to iron and are beautifully glossy when finished.

871. **To Save the Labour of Black-leading the Kitchen Range** all over every week, get a tin of Brunswick Black and thin down with three parts linseed oil and one part turpentine; mix well and apply with a flat paint brush to stone after all dust and soot, etc., has been removed. Leave to dry thoroughly before lighting a fire. The grate will look bright and cheerful, and only the front bars will need blackleading for quite three months. Bedroom and sittingroom grates all look like new with this treatment.

872. **To Clean Copper that has Worn Shabby,** such as fire-irons, etc., instead of the weekly metal polish drudgery, use preservene soap melted in very hot water, add some common whitening and wash the articles with a nice flannel cloth. Dry thoroughly and finish off with a good furniture paste. This will not only make the articles look like new, but they will last clean and bright for five or six weeks.

873. **To Clean Silver.**—Silver cleaned with rouge and methylated spirit resists tarnish and finger-marks longer than when ordinary whitening and water are used. The rouge and spirit may be mixed in a bottle all ready for use. Keep tightly corked.

874. **To Clean Windows.**—One teaspoonful of vinegar added to water when cleaning windows and mirrors, etc., bring a brilliant polish easy and quickly.

875. **To Clean Furniture Covered in Tapestry.**—A bowl of warm water (not *hot*), nail brush and cloths. Dip brush in water and rub preservene soap on till a good lather is obtained. Then brush the tapestry briskly till all dirt is loosened ; wipe with a wet cloth to get all soap off ; then rub dry with another cloth (dry). This will renovate the colours and make the tapestry quite fresh and clean and the articles cleaned will soon dry by an open window or out in the air.

876. **To Clean and Remove all Grease from Gas Stoves, Inside and Outside.**—Make a lather of preservene soap and with a soft cloth wash the sides and door and all parts that are dirty and the grease will quickly disappear, leaving the stove quite clean and sweet. If preferred the soap can be dipped in warm water and well rubbed on to a soft cloth till a lather is obtained. Then rub all parts well and wipe out with a damp cloth.

877. **An excellent home-made Distemper.**—Put 5 lbs. of whitewash into a pail, and add a tablespoonful of powdered alum and half a packet of soap powder. Slowly pour on enough cold water to cover it. Leave till the next day. Then, with your hands, work the soaked whiting into a smooth cream. Dissolve 1 lb. of size in a quart of water, when ready stir in, then add half-pint of flour paste, made with flour and water. Work all up carefully and add hot water till it is like a thick, smooth cream.

878. **A Cheap Powder for Cleaning Pans.**—For a good cheap powder for cleaning pans, stains on crockery, etc., take a packet of washing powder and half a pound of powdered pumice, mix well together and put in a tin for use.

879. **For Washing New Blankets.**—For washing new blankets, soak over-night in water to which two or three handsful of salt has been added ; wring out and put into a good preservene soap lather ; wring out and put into warm water in which an ounce of glycerine has been added. Your blankets will be quite as fluffy as when new.

880. **Knife Cleaning.**—Cover two pieces of wood with emery paper, turning well over the sides and secure by gum or nails. Place the one piece on top of the other, with the emery paper together. Nail the two ends. Slip the knife into the division, press lightly ; rub the knife once or twice and both sides will be cleaned at once.

881. **Carpet Cleaning.**—If you have a grass patch in the garden it is a great help when sweeping carpets. Lay the carpet face downwards on the damp grass, and drag first one way, then the other. This not only removes a good deal of the dust, but freshens the carpet.

882. **Ironing Hints**—If the ironing blanket is covered with two or three sheets of white paper (newspaper will do) and the articles ironed on this, they will not stick and it will give them a gloss equal to new—quite a laundry finish. A piece of sandpaper tacked to the end of the ironing board will be found very useful for cleaning irons. A little salt will remove starch from irons. Never allow irons to become red hot—as it roughens them and they never retain their heat afterwards. When ironing keep a paraffin duster handy to rub the irons. This will prevent irons sticking, and help them to retain their heat much longer.

883. **Washing-up.**—The task of washing-up, where a good deal has to be done, takes a deal of time and energy in the course of a day, much of which could be saved. For a small amount a detachable draining board can be obtained which will save many journeys backwards and forwards. A sink to be labour-saving should have draining boards

both sides, with shelves underneath and with this arrangement the work can be done without unnecessary walking.

884. **When Cooking Eggs and Rashers,** make use of a white glazed fire-proof dish in which lay the rashers and put in a hot gas oven. When they are nearly ready, break an egg on each one, close the oven door, and turn out the gas. In ten minutes both eggs and rashers are cooked perfectly and the dish being of good appearance can be brought direct to the table, thereby saving time in dishing up, labour in washing the frying pan, and gas which would be used all the time if cooked over a gas ring.

885. **Bedsteads.**—For **enamel** bedsteads use turpentine and water ; for **mahogany** bedsteads use equal parts of linseed oil, paraffin oil and vinegar and one tablespoonful of methylated spirits. Rub in sparingly and polish with a large soft duster. For **oak bedsteads** use linseed oil.

886. **To remove Tar Stains** from clothes rub well with lard as soon as the garment is stained. Afterwards wash out the greasy stain of the lard with hot water, to which has been added a teaspoonful of liquid ammonia. Use a little soap on a nail brush.

887. **Keep Spare Room Bed Aired,** by putting hot water bottles in it once a week. Put them in different spots each time. The bed is always ready for an unexpected guest.

888. **To Clean Glass.**—All glass if cleaned with salt and water lasts longer clean than other chemicals and gives a better polish. Be sure to let the salt water dry on the glass then rub off with a chamois leather.

889. **To Clean Copper Articles** which are very Soiled.— Copper articles which are very soiled are most easily cleaned with equal parts of vinegar and salt, after which rinse in warm water to remove acid and give final polish with soft cloth.

890. **To Prevent a Cake from Burning.**—If, when baking a cake, you place another cake tin the same size over it, your cake will not burn, and will bake much more evenly, and you can leave it without looking at it, until it has had sufficient time to bake.

891. **After the Day's Washing.**—After finishing the day's wash with preservene soap, and before you empty the boiling water out of the copper, put in the baking tins which have become brown from the fat, the pie-dishes and saucepans which have become stained from fruit and vegetables, leave in the boiling water about ten minutes; take out and rub with a ball of steel wool and they will become bright as new.

892. **To Clean Stained Hands.**—If as soon as you have prepared vegetables which stain the hands, such as potatoes, onions, carrots, etc., the hands are rubbed over with a squeeze of lemon-juice, the stain will at once disappear.

893. **Renovating Last Winter's Hats.**—Velour and felt hats can be made to look like new by the following simple process. Brush and beat the dust well out; then, if the hats are light in colour, rub well with stale pieces of bread until clean. In the meantime a small pan of boiling water should be got ready. Pour into the water a few drops of ammonia and add about $\frac{1}{2}$ oz. of preservene soap, finely shredded. Keep water boiling all the time and steam the hat, taking care not to scorch it. During this process the hat may be bent to the shape required.

894. **How to Rid a Room of Flies.**—Take a piece of galvanised fencing wire about two feet long; cover with bird-lime to about six inches from the top. Bend this into the shape of a hook, and hang to clothes-rack. To clean wire, put into the fire and burn off. When cold, cover again with bird-lime

895. **Brass Curtain Rods** that are discoloured and spoilt by verdigris can be renovated by scouring them with powdered pumice stone and turpentine, made into a paste. They can be polished with dry powder or with metal polish or rubbed with an oily rag.

896. **When Washing Paint,** use a partly worn loofah and soap. This gets in corners where a brush cannot get, and does not injure even the most delicate enamel.

897. **A Cake Hint.**—When baking a cake, especially for icing, make a large hole in the centre of the mixture. This makes it flat and saves time, as it is more easily iced.

898. **Preserving Pan Hint.**—Rub the bottom of your preserving pan with a little butter.

899. **Borax.**—Add a little to kitchen towels when washing. This makes them a good colour and eradicates grease and dirt.

900. **A Good Floor Polisher** can be made with a worn-out broom covered with various pieces of felt or tweed tacked on. It saves kneeling.

901. **To Store Silver.**—A little olive oil rubbed over silver before it is put away will prevent it becoming tarnished. When required for use, wash in warm soapy water and dry thoroughly.

902. **Olive Oil for Cleaning the Hands.**—Olive oil is good for cleaning the hands. Rub well into the hands and well lather with soap.

903. **Kid Glove Hint.**—Before putting on new kid gloves lay them in the folds of a damp towel to prevent cracking.

904. **To Make Old Curtains Last.**—Dip small pieces in your starch ; place evenly over the rent, then press with a hot iron and the repair is complete.

905. **To Clean Enamelled Tins,** pans, etc., scrub with preservene Soap and salt.

906. **To Remove Rust Stains from Linen.**—Rub with fresh cut lemon and salt ; then wash and dry.

907. **To Bleach Clothes.**—Dip into water, then spread on green grass. Repeat several times.

908. **To Remove Tarnish Stains.**—Monkey soap and ammonia will remove tarnish stains from brasses easily.

909. **To Remove Dye Stains from Ivory-backed Mirrors.** To remove dye stains from ivory-backed mirrors, rub firmly with powdered Vim.

910. **To Remove Ink Stains.**—Spread the yolk of a new laid egg over the stain. Let it remain for about ten minutes, then plunge the fabric into boiling water and allow it to soak for a short time. Take it out, rub the marks thoroughly, when all traces of ink, whether stains of long or short duration, will have entirely disappeared.

911. **If There is No Bath in the House.**—If there is no bathroom in the house, fix rubber hose to the scullery tap and carry it through the windows into the room above to fill a tub.

912. **To Have Hot Water in the Morning.**—Tack a blanket or sacking coat round the cistern.

913. **When Re-Papering a Room,** the hardest job is scraping off the old paper. Shut the room up with a tub of water on a gas-ring or stove, and half your work is done, the steam loosening the paper.

914. **To Remove a Rusty Screw,** heat it with a red-hot poker. Screw it tighter first, and this will loosen it.

915. **To Free a Stopped Sink.**—Use salt and soda, and then pour down a kettleful of boiling water. Or, half-fill your sink with water, and placing the palm of your hand over the hole, work it up and down.

916. **To Clean a Carpet Rapidly.**—A carpet may be well and rapidly cleaned with hot bran and a stiff brush.

917. **How to Find the South by Your Watch.**—You may save many a step by knowing how to find the South by your watch (in England). Point the hour hand to the sun, halfway between the hour and twelve o'clock (in the nearest direction) is due south.

918. **Handy Measures.**—A halfpenny is one inch in diameter ; three new pennies weigh 1 oz. ; one tablespoonful of flour, sugar, etc., equals 1 oz. ; one tumbler holds half a pint.

919. **To Tie Jam-pots Quickly and Securely.**—To tie jam-pots quickly and securely, use wet string, which shrinks when dry, and so holds. Make a loop nearly at one end of the string, slip the other end through and take round the pot again.

920. **How to Prevent Milk from Boiling Over.**—Smear a little butter round the upper part of the saucepan, and your milk will not boil over, so you need not watch it. Or a funnel in the pan, with the top well above milk line, will answer the same purpose.

921. **Saucepan Hint.**—An inverted saucer at the bottom of your saucepan will save the contents from burning.

922. **To Avoid Lumps in Salt.**—Avoid lumps in salt (from dampness) by keeping a bean or two in the jar. These absorb all moisture.

923. **To Cure Burns.** To prevent a blister after a burn smear with a paste of whitening and water.

924. **When Bottling Fruit** put two cross-wise bits of tape under the cork, to remove it easily.

925. **To Save much Cleaning in the Kitchen.**—To save much cleaning of the kitchen-table, cover it with linoleum fastened at the corners. Or have a piece of board or cardboard to fit, covered with American cloth. This is much neater and more handy than newspapers.

926. **How to Keep Your Larder Clean and Cool.**—Have slate on your larder shelves. This is cool and easy to keep clean.

927. **Stove Hint.** When a fireplace has been out of use, a bundle of straw burnt in, will drive all damp and stagnant air up the chimney.

928. **Before Weeding,** or other dirty work, scrape your nails full of soap and rub cream on your hands. The dirt will then easily wash off the surface.

929. **If a Plant Needs Frequent Watering** sink a sloped flower-pot in the earth so that the hole in the pot points to the plant's roots. Fill the pot with water in the morning and it will keep the earth damp, filtering through very slowly.

930. **To Whiten Your Doorsteps,** melt 2 ozs. of powdered glue over the fire in an old tin, with $\frac{1}{2}$ pint water. Stir in 4 ozs. of whitening and a lump of salt as big as a walnut. Paint the steps on a dry day— and only a brush will be needed in case of a muddy footstep.

931. **To Avoid Moth in Your Carpet,** sweep every two or three weeks with crushed rock-salt. This will also brighten the colours.

932. **To Clean Silver Quickly.**—Silver is cleaned quickly if soaked first in potato-water. For salt stains, rub with damp salt ; it works like magic. Silver will keep bright if soaked once a week in strong borax solution. The water used should be near boiling. Put away unused silver. Wrap it in linen and then roll in green baize. Newspaper also is excellent. Something in the printer's ink prevents rust.

933. **When Ribbons Get Wet on a Hat.**—Iron them by heating a tablespoon and pressing it into the bows the concave side.

934. **An Eiderdown Quilt may be Washed with very little trouble** by flaking one bar of preservene soap and making a lather in water comfortably hot to the hand. Soak the quilt a short time and then squeeze the dirt out gently. No rubbing needed. Rinse in warm water ; squeeze dry, but neither wring not mangle. Hang out to drip, and when dry, beat it with a cane to divide the feathers. (The Swiss beat a " duvet " with a stick daily, when bed-making.)

935. **To Wash Valuable Lace.**—Put it in a jam jar with cold water and soap jelly (made by scraping preservene soap and boiling in a little water). Put the jar in a pan of water with lid on, and boil two to three hours.

936. **To Keep Brick Floors a Nice Red Colour,** add a small quantity of paraffin to the pail of water each time the floor is washed.

937. **A Quick Way to Scrape Potatoes** which have been dug up a few days, is to cover them with hot water in which a small lump of soda has been dissolved. Let them remain in this for ten minutes, and the skins will come off as easily as if fresh dug up and will not stain the fingers.

938. **A Good Way to Wash a Chamois Leather** is to make a nice soapy lather with a piece of preservene, wash the leather in this and hang up to dry without rinsing. It will dry as soft as when new.

939. **For Washing Day.**—In the winter pop your pegs in the oven for a few minutes before hanging out the clothes. The warm pegs prevent that icy numbing feeling in the fingers.

940. **To Dust Old China.**—A silk handkerchief will be most useful for dusting old china, the silk being softer where delicate handling is required. For washing china make a nice lather with warm water and preservene soap jelly. One or two feathers are necessary where filigree china is concerned. Work into the design with the feathers to get the dust out of crevices. Allow to drain, then polish off with soft silk.

941. **The Quickest Way to Clean Windows.**—Moisten a cloth well with paraffin oil and clean with it as many windows as required. Then go back to the first window and polish it with a soft dry cloth. This polishes very quickly and brilliantly, and keeps flies from settling on or near the windows.

942. **Soup-making Hint. Bones required** for making soup will keep fresh and in good condition for several days if they are baked for a few minutes in a hot oven.

943. **Artificial " Hands " to Help Wind Wool.**—Two celluloid or enamelled wire " hands " fixed at an angle to small wood or metal blocks lined with rubber or felt, which would clamp on to a table or windowsill, at a convenient distance apart for folks who have no one to hold their wool. The " hands " would need to be about the width of a woman's hand and shaped (in profile) something like a hat peg and placed on the small blocks at the angle

one usually holds one's hands when helping to wind wool. The tops of the " fingers " should be slightly pliable so that the pressure of the wool would allow it to slip over the top without the whole skein coming off. The two " hands " need to be very firm but not clumsy and the felt or rubber would prevent slipping and scratching on the table.

944. **Grass Stains.**—Grass stains can be removed by covering the spot with equal parts of tartaric acid and salt moistened with a little water and then allowed to dry in the sun. Glycerine rubbed on the stain an hour before washing in warm water will often remove it entirely.

945. **To Prevent Ink from Staining.**—When ink is spilt, quickly wet with milk, and inkstain will wash out quite easily.

946. **To Remove Sea-Water Stains.**—Dark blue and black materials easily become stained with sea-water, but vinegar will usually restore colour, if it is rubbed on with a piece of the same material. It is best to wear only light-coloured washing frocks at the seaside.

947. **To Keep Chimneys Clear.**—Burn potato peelings mixed with salt at least once a week in your grate. Such a glaze will form on the inside of your chimney that it cannot get clogged with soot, so is not likely to get on fire.

948. **Brooms and Brushes** last much longer when dipped weekly into a pail of boiling soap suds. After washing day with preservene soap the remaining suds in the boiler answer the purpose quite well.

949. **Boys' Suits.**—When cutting out little suits for boys, there are always small pieces left over. Place one such piece across each knee and elbow, between the lining and material. When the top material is worn, cut it away and darn neatly ; also treat the trousers seat in the same way. It saves the trouble of affixing patches and expense of matching same.

950. **A Disinfectant Hint.**—As a disinfectant during Influenza epidemics add a few drops of Eucalyptus Oil to every pail of hot water, for household purposes. For cleaning rooms and staircases this solution is a good preventative. Brooms and brushes dipped in Eucalyptus Oil and water can also be used for sweeping carpets.

951. **Banishing Flies.**—Frequent examination of cupboards where food is stored, and the washing of windows and frames where flies settle, with a strong disinfectant water, will prevent flies from accumulating. As much refuse as possible should be burnt. Cedar-wood oil, obtainable from any chemist, placed on cotton-wool and left about the rooms will prove effective; stinging-nettles, elder, cloves and the common oxeye daisy are used very effectually to keep away flies.

952. **Kindling a Fire.**—After cleaning out all dust and ashes from the grate, place in the bottom two or three crumpled balls of newspaper. These form the core of the pyramid and serve as a support to the pieces of firewood or twists of paper. The firewood or twists are next arranged round the core, standing up on end with the tops meeting like a pyramid or tent. Then pieces of coal are put round the base to keep things in place. Small light pieces of coal and cinder are next lightly arranged up the sides and a light applied to the core. Do not bump or throw on the coal heavily, or failure will result. Needless to say all the kindling materials must be thoroughly dry.

953. **A Washing Day Hint.**—When tablecloths get tea spilt on them, soak them for a few hours in the usual way, adding a little borax to the water, and also put a teaspoonful of borax in the copper when boiling them. The stains will disappear almost immediately, and the clothes will be much whiter.

954. **Labour Saver.**—Half a pint of paraffin mixed with half a pint of ordinary brown vinegar is a wonderful labour-saving cleanser and polisher. It is excellent for polishing all kinds of furniture without much effort, and is splendid also for cleaning tiles, marble, linoleum, oilcloth, as well as for cleaning any kind of paint work.

955. **Make Your Own Nightlights.**—The best fat for this purpose is made by saving the drippings or small ends of candles, improving it by shredding a little white wax into it. Melt this and pour it into the bottom of pill or other empty boxes. When cool, but not quite set, drop a wick made of a twist of cotton into the centre of each one.

956. **Washing Day Hint.**—When dampening your clothes for ironing, use a small bottle nearly filled with water, and cut a small groove in one side of the cork. This method sprinkles the clothes more evenly and quickly, and does not make so much mess on the table as the old-fashioned way of sprinkling with the fingers.

957. **Fall of Soot on a Carpet.**—If soot falls on a carpet, blow it off gently with a pair of bellows. Mix some salt and bran together, and spread it thickly on the place where the soot has fallen. Brush well backwards and forwards with a hard brush. Sweep off the salt and bran, and the carpet will be quite clean.

958. **Damp Salt as Fire Extinguisher.** Damp salt kept in readiness, and thrown on a fire in case of accident, will extinguish it immediately.

959. **Icing a Cake.**—A little flour sprinkled over the top of a cake will prevent the icing sugar running over the sides.

960. **To Remove Fruit Stains from Linen, etc.**—Place a teaspoonful of sugar on the stain, then boil.

961. **To Remove Scorch Marks.**—Boil half a pint of vinegar, 2 ozs. of preservene soap, 2 ozs. of Fuller's earth, and an onion (chopped) for ten minutes. Strain and when cold spread on marks and allow to dry.

962. **To Remove Grease from Carpets.**—Put a tablespoonful of ammonia into a pint of hot water and scrub the grease spots with a brush. Rub dry with a cloth, then make a paste with Fuller's Earth and cold water. Lay over spots ; leave till dry, then brush off. If very old, the paste may have to be repeated.

963. **To Clean Inside Coat Collars.**—Grate one tablespoonful preservene soap, rub dry on soiled part of collar, leave two hours, brush off, with clean clothes-brush or nail brush, then with soft cloth wrung very dry in hot, clean water, until dirt is removed. Rub until nearly dry with clean dry cloth. Press with hot iron.

964. **For Aching Feet and Ankles.**—Make a solution of two tablespoonsful preservene, half a gallon hot water. Bathe feet in same twenty minutes. Rub dry with a soft cloth, then rub feet well with a little castor oil.

965. **Fire Lighters.**—Satisfactory fire lighters are difficult to obtain, but the following home-made ones are excellent. Take a sheet of newspaper fold lightly in half, roll up, twist the roll lightly in the centre, or tie with string. Then dip in melted paraffin wax or kerosene. The former dries in less than a minute, the latter takes longer, and should be dried out of doors. A stock of such fire lighters are a boon and save the cost of firewood.

966. **Taking Ink Stains from Carpet.**—This applies to freshly-spilt ink. First take up the greater part of ink with blotting paper, afterwards rubbing in salt with damp rag. Repeat with fresh rag till all traces are gone. Afterwards brush with powdered borax, when it will be found perfectly clean.

967. **When Washing Men's Greasy Overalls,** all the laborious scrubbing and rubbing is saved by soaking them first in a nice preservene lather for a short time, then wash out, and put them through starch (when this is done with for other clothes) which helps the dirt to slip out quite easily the next time they are washed.

968. **Labour Saved in Cleaning Brasses, etc., in Damp Weather.**—More than half the labour will be saved in the cleaning of brasses, etc., in damp weather, if after cleaning you rub over with a cloth smeared slightly with vaseline.

969. **Ink can be Removed from the Most Delicate-looking Carpet** if the stain is washed immediately with warm milk, plenty of which must be used and rubbed well into the carpet with a piece of clean flannel. The milk should be poured on the *stain*, not the flannel.

970. **A Simple and Easy Way to Polish Furniture** is to wring a piece of flannel out nearly dry in warm water before putting on the polish. Then proceed in the usual way and polish with a soft duster. This saves labour in rubbing and leaves the furniture smoothly and brightly polished, without being smeary.

971. **A Stocking Hint.**—To prevent black cotton stockings from losing their colour in the wash, soak them all night in warm weak suds and wash in warm water to which a teaspoonful of turpentine has been added, using plain soap. Rinse well in cold water.

972. **A Wool-winding Tip.**—Next time you want to wind wool yourself, remember this tip. Stand two flatirons on the table, and put the wool over the handles.

973. **To Clean Water Bottles or Decanters.**—Tear up small pieces of newspaper and put in and then fill up with water. Let them stay for five minutes and then give a good shake. You will find all stains disappear and the bottles beautifully bright.

974. **To Remove Mildew.**—Soak the affected garment in buttermilk, then boil in the usual way in soap.

975. **To Clean Knives Easily.**—Rub with Monkey Brand after washing.

976. **To Save Cleaning Grates when Not in Use.**—Brush over with Stovo, and to keep the steelwork from rusting rub lightly with vaseline.

977. **To Keep Flies Out of a Room.**—Hang up a bunch of elderflower.

978. **Pleasure Given when Ironing,** after washing with preservene soap, is to run the hot iron over the soap-wrapper which makes the iron smooth and clean ; no sticking or soiling after.

979. **When Jam-making, Use White Tissue Paper** for the caps to cover. Just brush wet with milk over the jars of hot jam ; will dry stiff as a bladder. No paste or string required.

980. **To Keep Brasses from Tarnishing Quickly.**—After having been cleaned, apply on piece of clean flannel a little furniture Ronuk and polish again. This can be used on china ornaments to keep bright and clean, after being washed.

981. **To Clean Dirty Furniture.**—Two tablespoonsful of vinegar in half a pint of lukewarm water. Damp a clean old stocking with the mixture and rub the furniture all over. When dry you will need less labour and polish to give a lasting brilliant shine. The same method applies to mirrors.

982. **Peeling Onions and Shalots for Pickling.**—Put the onions in a large bowl and cover with boiling water. Let them stand for five minutes. Put them in another bowl and cover with cold water. You will find they will peel easier and the eyes will not smart at all.

983. **To Wash Coloured Stockings.**—Delicate coloured stockings should be soaked in a pail of water containing a quarter of a pint of turpentine, wrung out and dried before washing in the ordinary manner. This procedure sets the colour and the stockings may be washed without fear of fading.

984. **To Clean Stained and Grained and Varnished Paint.**— Use linseed oil on a flannel and rub well in.

985. **To Wash New Coloured Jumpers, etc.**—Soak them in a bucket of cold water with a tablespoonful of turpentine in. This sets the colours. Then wash in the usual way.

986. **For Washing-up Silver.**—If when washing-up silver, preservene soap is put into the water, it will never require cleaning.

987. **To Clean Lampshades.**—Put a small portion of soap jelly into a basin of hot water. Dip the shade up and down several times in the lather. Rinse well, and hang up to dry in the open-air if possible.

988. **To Remove Grease Spots from Floors and Tables** without scrubbing, and with cold water, make the floor or table wet with houseflannel, then rub well the part to be cleaned with any good soap, wipe off, and dirt and grease will have disappeared as if by magic.

989. **Starching Hint.**—Before putting your clothes into the preservene lather you have prepared put some of the soapy water on one side and use the next day to make your starch with. Your things will iron up much better than if the starch is mixed with clear water.

990. **Care of Hands.**—Before beginning rough work, or even dusting, well rub into the skin a non-greasy cream,

taking care to rub same into cuticle round nails.   When the work is finished, well soak the hands in soapy lather, and you will find no dirt has got into the skin.

991.  **Cooking Hint.**—Sprinkle the top of your stove with salt before you begin to fry.   The grease from pan will then not mark the stove, neither will there be any smell of burnt fat.   The stove can later be rubbed over with newspaper and will be quite clean.

992.  **Cleaning Enamel Ware.**  Soda cracks enamel.  A saucepan will soon burn and crack if it is washed in soda water.   Save used lemons, put a little cinder dust into the saucepan and rub with the lemon.   It quickly cleans off any burnt food.   A burnt saucepan should at once be filled with cold water and left awhile before cleaning.

993.  **Removing Stains.**—Salts of  lemon is poisonous, therefore dangerous.   If a little pure glycerine is poured over stains before the article is washed, and allowed to remain at least an hour, the stain will come out in the wash. This also applies to dresses, etc., that are stained through perspiration.

994.  **Ironing Hint to Preserve Sheets, Tablecloths, etc.**— These are always folded into the same folds when ironed. In time these folds wear thin, and it is necessary to darn them.   At the first sign of wear, cut off about half an inch in width from one side of the worn article.   The folds will then not come in the same places.

995.  **To Sweep a Carpet.**—Shredded newspaper, soaked in a bucket of water, then squeezed out and sprinkled over a carpet that has to be swept, will bring up the colours better than tea leaves.   If tea leaves are used they should be previously rinsed in several waters, otherwise they may leave a stain.

996. **Quick Lighting of Fires.**—Do not throw away used matches or night lights. Keep an old biscuit box for the purpose of storing match-boxes containing used matches and night lights. These will help to kindle a fire quickly.

997. **Cleaning Table Glass.**—Bottles that have had milk in them should not at first be washed in hot water, but well rinsed in cold water, then half fill with soapy hot water, shake well, and then again rinse they will be quite clear, and have no greasy marks left.

998. **Sewing Machine Hint.**—When about to machine muslin or lace, tack a piece of tissue paper over it and then machine. The paper is easily torn away, and the machine needle will not catch in the muslin or lace.

999. **Hint for Kitchen Floor.**—Should you decide to cover the floor with linoleum, have an old carpet, no matter how worn, put down under it. This answers a three-fold purpose. (1) The floor is warmer. (2) Feet do not get so cold in winter. (3) The lino lasts longer. Never drench with water the lino when washing it, but dip a soft scrubbing brush into soapy water, scrub quickly, but lightly, wash off soapy water, and dry thoroughly with dry cloth. Lino so treated will wear for years.

1000. **To Remove Stains from Glass Bottles, Decanters, etc.**—To remove stains in glass bottles, decanters, tumblers, or any kind of glass dishes, etc., a little coal dust and cold water, shake well until stains are removed, then rinse with lather made with soap and hot water. Rinse with cold water and polish.

1001. **To Clean Straw Matting** use a little salt in water.

1002. **When Plucking Fowls,** first pour *boiling* water over them and let them soak for a few minutes. By doing this the feathers come off in a quarter the usual time, all insects are killed, and the feathers do not fly about.

1003. **After Removing Stains from the Carpet.**—After having rubbed a stain off the carpet with soap and water, dab the wet part with vinegar to bring back the original colour of the carpet.

1004. **Cutting Mint for Sauce.**—Pick off leaves, place on chopping board and sprinkle with fine sugar and chop. It will only take a few seconds.

1005. **Escaped Parrot.**—Never chase a parrot to frighten him. Get a walking stick and hold before his feet. He will soon hop on ; then gently lift stick to cage door, and in polly goes, thus saving time and labour.

1006. **To Keep Brasswork Bright.**—Brasswork can be kept beautifully bright by occasionally rubbing with salt and vinegar.

1007. **The Care of the Hands.**—If the hands are stained after picking red currants, rinse first in cold water before washing with preservene soap and warm water. A busy housewife need never have soiled and unsightly hands if little hints of this kind are followed. Always use a good cream daily on face, neck, hands and arms.

1008. **For Cleaning Tin Utensils,** such as pails, cans, etc., which have become stained and dirty, turpentine applied first before cleaning will quickly remove all dirt and grease, leaving utensil quite clean.

1009. **Stains from Fresh or Cooked Fruit.**—Cover the stain with pure glycerine, leave all night, and wash and boil as usual the next day.

1010. **A Good Cement.**—To fill holes in the wall made by nails, or round window frames, where plaster has given way, tear up an old newspaper into a bowl with a few scraps of soap, cover with boiling water, squeeze out ;

mix with a little cold potato ; work with the hands till it holds well together, then press well into holes. When dry mix a little soap with whitening and rub over. This will last longer than ordinary plaster and will not break away.

1011. **For Insect Bites.**—Take a piece of soap, dip into cold water, then rub the wet surface lightly upon the bite. The irritation immediately stops.

1012. **Stove Cleaning.**—Before cleaning a stove, if you are not in the habit of wearing gloves, rub your hands well over with soap. This will prevent them getting ingrained as so often is the case after stove-cleaning.

1013. **When Washing Muslin or Lace Curtains.** When washing muslin, lace or net curtains, before putting them in water, fold them neatly into a small compass and keep them folded until they are washed and dried. This keeps them from tearing with the weight of the water and they last much longer. If very smoky or soiled, soak them over-night in cold soda and water, then wash in the usual way

1014. **To Clean Tennis Balls.**—Scrub well with hot water and soap. Rinse and dry in the open-air. This method is excellent and quite harmless to the rubber lining, the balls when dry being like new.

1015. **To Keep Brass Articles Clean for about Six Months.** —Clean the brass with any kind of good metal polish and then apply the following with a soft brush : 1 oz. pure white shellac dissolved in $\frac{1}{4}$ pint methylated spirits. This forms a transparent film on the brass. Taps on stoves which become greasy can be wiped over with soap and water without removing this film.

1016.   **For Grease Stains.**—To clean crepe-de-chine dress material of oil lay a little carbonate of magnesia on the stains ; hold it in front of the fire for a minute, and then gently rub off with cotton-wool. Nobody can see the stain.

1017.   **For Removing Paint Stains from Glass.**—Hot vinegar is an excellent thing for removing paint stains from glass.

1018.   **When Cooking Fruit.**—If a pinch of salt is added when cooking fruit, only half the quantity of sugar need be used.

1019.   **Saucepans in which Porridge has been boiled**, or anything which sticks to the bottom, should be filled with cold water directly and then stood on the side of the stove where it is not hot.  It will be found that the whole will come easily from the bottom of its own accord in about half an hour.

1020.   **To Clean Ostrich Feathers.**—Get a bowl of luke-warm water and a piece of preservene soap.  Put the feathers into the water and well soap them, rubbing them with the tops of the fingers until they look clean.  Then rinse well several times in cold water.  Dry them well in a clean towel by squeezing.  Do not wring them.  Then beat them on a clean table.

1021.   **To Remove Scorch Marks.**—Boil 2 ozs. soap with half a pint of vinegar and an onion chopped fine, for ten minutes.  Strain, and when cold spread on mark, allowing to dry.  Afterwards washing in the usual way.

1022.   **To Blacken Brown Boots.**—Rub well with a raw potato, and then apply black polish in the usual way.

**1023. To Preserve Lemons.**—If half a lemon is wanted for flavouring, place the unused half on a plate and cover it with a glass. This will exclude the air and preserve the lemon.

**1024. Mirrors and Picture Glasses** should be cleaned with a pad of tissue paper, sprinkled with methylated spirit. The result will be a brilliant and lasting polish, and one that will save you hours of labour.

**1025. Rusty Curtain Hooks.**—Curtain hooks that have become rusty will be found to go into the curtain quite easily if first stuck into a piece of soap.

**1026. To Get Rid of Mice.**—Plaster up their holes with a mixture of soap and pepper.

**1027. Flies.**—To keep flies out of a room, soak some small pieces of sponge in warm water, then sprinkle with a few drops of oil of lavender. Place them about the room, out of sight, just inside ornaments or behind pictures, etc. The flies do not like the smell, which is not unpleasant.

**1028. To Save Gas.**—To save gas get a piece of sheet iron large enough to cover the top of the stove, and use this for cooking. You will find that one burner alight will be able to keep two or three pans going at once.

**1029. To Polish a Stove.**—Blacklead the stove in the usual manner. But instead of polishing it with a brush use a crushed newspaper. This is a much easier and more effective way than brushing.

**1030. To Remove Tea, Coffee or Other Stains from Silk or Delicate Garments.**—Shred half a bar of preservene soap into about one and a half pints cold water. Boil until dissolved and when cold place in the stained garment, steep overnight, when it will be found that all traces have

disappeared and without injury to the material.   Silk and
crepe-de-chine especially.   I have specially proved this to be
so.

1031.   **A Hint after Darning.**—After darning from a new
card of mending wool, I always nick the top of card with
scissors and slip the end of the wool in.   This avoids looking
for the end, which is very annoying with dark wool.

1032.   **Reviving Colours in Faded Blouses, Ribbons, etc.**—
After washing, blouses, ribbons, etc., dissolve a teaspoonful
of tartaric acid in cold water and rinse each article well in
it.   No matter how faded a thing is this does wonders.

1033.   **Shred Runner Beans** on the ordinary potato
peeler.   Not only is it quicker and easier, but the fine
cut beans are delicious.

1034.   **If You Wrap Your Furs** entirely in newspaper
before putting them away for the summer, it will keep
them absolutely free from moths.

1035.   **When Chopping Suet**, try sprinkling the knife
with a little ground rice and you will have no trouble.

1036.   **To Test an Oven for Baking Cakes.**—Throw a
pinch of flour on the bottom of the oven, and if it is too
hot the flour will burn and smoke in half a minute.   If just
right, it will go brown in about two minutes, but not burn.

1037.   **When stewing fruit** put a quarter teaspoonful
of bicarbonate of soda into fruit when stewing.   This will
save a third of the sugar usually required.

1038.   **Doyleys** are apt to go all sorts of funny shapes
unless thay are ironed in just the right way.   Do not iron
from side to side, whatever you do.   Pull the doyley in
shape as it lies on the ironing sheet, and pat it down
smoothly with your hands.   Then iron from the centre

outwards, using a small iron.   Of course, you must place the doyley on the ironing sheet, with the right side downward.

1039.   **A Brilliant Gloss for Linen.**—Pound 2 ozs. of gum arabic to a powder and put it in a jug.   Pour over it $1\frac{1}{2}$ pints of boiling water ; cover the jug and let it remain all night. Next morning pour the liquid carefully from the dregs into a clean bottle ; cork and keep for use.   A tablespoonful of this stirred into a pint of starch made in the usual way will give a splendid gloss.

1040.   **To Remove Perspiration Stain.**—If any garment is stained under the arms, put it to soak for half an hour in warm water to which a little ammonia has been added (use no soap, as it sets the stain).   Then wring, and if the mark has not quite gone, squeeze a little lemon juice on to it, and rinse in clean warm water.   Afterwards wash in the ordinary way.

1041.   **Feather Pillows.**—When refilling feather pillows crush a small block of camphor and sprinkle among the feathers, as it helps to preserve them and makes the pillow feel cool and refreshing to the head.

1042.   **A Hanging Meat Safe.**—Cut out a round of thick cardboard.   Buy half a yard of double-width, strong, coarse net.   Sew two sides of the net strongly together, hem the top, and thread a tape through it.   Then sew the bottom round the cardboard, and you will have a bag of net with a firm cardboard bottom, on which a plate of meat can rest.   The bag should be hung in a draught.

1043.   **To Remove Match Marks** from a painted wall, rub first with a slice of lemon and then with a clean cloth dipped in whitening.   Then wash off the surface with warm water and soap and wipe with a clean cloth wrung dry.

1044. **To Make Cotton-wool Safe.**—Lay the large sheets of cotton wool, folded just as purchased, in a bath with about two gallons of water and 1 lb. of alum. Leave it for twelve hours, then hang up to drip and dry. It can then be used as required without danger.

1045. **Nursing Hint.**—You cannot be too careful with bottles containing poison or " not to be taken " mixtures. They should not be stored in the regular medicine chest but locked away out of reach. When, in case of illness, it is necessary to keep a bottle containing some poisonous mixture handy, do not stand it anywhere near the medicine " to be taken." And, to make quite sure that the bottle cannot be mistaken for a harmless one, tie a little bell round the neck—the little jingly things that are sewn on children's reins will do—to ring a warning the moment the bottle is touched.

1046. **To Strengthen Gas Mantles.**—In order to make incandescent mantles hard and unbreakable, except when considerable force is used, dissolve a teaspoonful of sal ammoniac in a cupful of vinegar and saturate the mantle with this solution before burning. Let the mantle dry before using. You will find the light much brighter, and the mantle will not get blackened.

1047. **To Frost a Window.**—Many people have a window which they would like barred to the gaze of passers-by. This can be managed by crystallising the window as follows : Take a jam pot one-third full of gum arabic, and add a little hot water. Let this soak for some hours, and when the gum has quite dissolved, add the same quantity of Epsom salts. Then stand the jam-pot in a basin of hot water and stir well until the salts have quite dissolved, and then apply the mixture quickly to the glass with a camel-hair brush. The effect is like crystallised ground glass, and whilst light is admitted, no one can see through it.

1048.  **To Clean Ceilings.**—A solution of 1 oz. of alum to one quart of water washed over a ceiling will clean it, and will also prevent it from peeling.

1049.  **To Prevent Soiling of Mattresses.**—For the care of bedrooms a large clean apron should be worn by the bedmaker.  If she has much housework to do, a pair of white cotton sleeves to be slipped on before making beds will be found a great assistance in preventing bed linen from becoming soiled.  All mattresses should either have cotton cases or strips of white calico tacked over their sides.  By these simple means, mattresses may be preserved as good as new for many years, but without this care mattresses soon become soiled.  These articles can be easily and quickly washed with soap.

1050.  **A Dusting Hint.**—Many housewives when dusting shake their duster out of the window every little while, which is a great loss of time.  Here is a swift and clean, method of dusting.  Add a little vinegar to a basin of lukewarm water.  Wet a chamois leather in the basin and rub the furniture with it.  Rinse the leather in the water to remove the dust which adheres to it.  The furniture will possess a delightful freshness, and the vinegar imparts such a beautiful gloss that polishing becomes a waste of time.

1051.  **Children's Pinafores.**—Even while comparatively new, children are apt to tear the pinafores just under the arm.  To obviate this annoyance, sew round the inside of the underarm of every new pinafore a small bit of tape. This is a great support, saves labour in mending and makes the garment wear much longer.

1052.  **An Easy Way to Take a Pattern of any Made-up Garment** is to place a piece of thin paper upon the table and lay the garment upon it—smoothing out all creases.  Pin the paper all over one half of the garment, then with a hat

pin prick from the wrong side of the garment all round the
seam right through to the paper.  Cut the paper along
pricked marks and when you have this half of the pattern
correct the other can be cut from it.

1053.  **When Machining Seams.**—Always tack seams
before machining, however simple they may appear.  This
will prevent one side becoming longer than the other,
especially when the material is cut on the cross.

1054.  **Before Baking Potatoes,** let them stand in hot
water for fifteen minutes.  They will require only half the
time for baking, are more mealy and palatable, and if they
are baked in a gas oven, the saving in gas is considerable.

1055.  **A Quick Way to Clean Currants** when making
cakes is to put the fruit into a colander with a sprinkling
of flour and rub it round a few times with your hand.  It is
surprising how quickly the stalks are separated and come
through the small holes.

1056.  **Fish May be Scaled Much Easier** by first dipping
it into boiling water for a minute.

1057.  **When Making Pastry**, melt the lard or dripping
slightly and beat to a cream before adding the flour.  Only
half the usual quantity of shortening will be required if
this is done.

1058.  **To Separate the White from the Yolk of an Egg.**—
Very frequently when separating the whites from the yolks
of eggs, the yolk becomes broken and falls into the white.
To prevent this, dip a cloth in warm water, ring it dry and
touch the yolk with the corner of it, and the yolk will
adhere to the cloth and may easily be removed.

1059.  **A Windy Day Starch Hint.**—A spoonful of salt
added while making starch will help to retain the stiffness
of the linen on a windy day.

1060. **To Prevent a Skin Forming on Starch.**—If a cloth is placed over a basin of freshly-made starch, no skin will form on the top.

1061. **Starch for a Bruise.**—A little dry starch—moistened with cold water and laid on the injured part, will prevent the skin discolouring after a bruise or fall. It also keeps down swelling.

1062. **To Remove Scorch Marks, etc.**—A little bicarbonate of soda mixed to a paste with cold water will remove scorch marks, perspiration, and other stains from white silk.

1063. **A Varnished Floor** should not be washed with hot water; a cloth wrung out in lukewarm water is best and each bit must be dried as it is washed.

1064. **Potatoes Baked in Their Skins** will be dry and mealy if a small piece is cut off the end to allow the steam to escape in cooking.

1065. **Buying Fish.**—Medium-sized fish are better than very large ones. The gills and the eyes should be bright. When buying flat fish look at both sides. In plaice the spots should be a vivid red. Cut fish should have flesh of a firm appearance and a close grain.

1066. **When Whitening Shoes.**—Milk used instead of water, for whitening shoes will prevent the whitening coming off on your clothes.

1067. **A Simple Cold Cure.**—A cup of hot milk to which has been added a teaspoonful of glycerine, makes an excellent remedy for a cold.

1068. **To restore Worn Emery Paper.**—Worn emery paper will regain much of its former rough surface if placed in a warm oven for a few minutes.

1069. **To Prevent a New Frying-pan from Warping,** wipe with a hot wet cloth, thoroughly dry it, cover inside the pan with melted fat, and let it boil gently for two minutes.

1070. **A Cold in the Head** may be relieved by putting a few pieces of camphor in a jug of hot water and inhaling the fumes.

1071. **When Marking Linen.**—If you first write the name with a blacklead pencil and then write over this with the ink, you will find that the pencil prevents the ink from running and looking most unsightly. Use a new nib each time.

1072. **Use Up Old Linen Collars.**—A good way to use up old collars is to cut them up and make them into luggage labels. They are much stronger than paper ones, and can be cut to any shape or size.

1073. **Blacklead is an Excellent Lubricator.**—Try the tip of a lead pencil on a squeaking door-hinge, and notice the result.

1074. **For Baby's Bonnet.**—To have fresh rosettes and strings for baby's bonnet at a moment's notice, embroider an eyelet at each corner of the bonnet where the ribbons are usually sewed. Have in hand a supply of small rosettes with ends attached to serve for strings. Slip the end through the eyelets and the bonnet is ready to tie. If the ribbons become soiled or a different colour is required, the change may be made instantly and no time wasted in taking off old ribbons and putting on new ones.

1075. **A Dusting Apron** is a most useful adjunct to the busy housewife. It should have a broad band containing a long pocket for the feather duster, another for the cloth, and one for the whisk broom.

1076. **For Large Shoes that Slip at the Heel.**—Glue a shaped piece of velvet to the inside of the heel, and it will cling to the stocking.

1077. **To Save Trouble in Packing.**—Always keep a list, either in your trunk or travelling bag, of those things which you will need while you are away from home. Half the labour of packing is saved by knowing exactly what you have to pack.

1078. **Potatoes** are apt to boil away if they are not constantly watched. Try this way next time. Strain off as much of the moisture as you can, and shake the pan over the fire for a second or so. Turn the " spoiled " potatoes into a perfectly clean cloth, fold over, take hold firmly of both ends, and gently—very gently—wring in opposite directions until all the moisture is out. You will now have a fine white ball of mealy potatoes instead of a watery mash.

1079. **A Useful Hint that May Save Your Life.**—If by any chance fat or grease of any description gets on fire in the oven, or over the fire, do not attempt to carry it out or put water on it. Quickly get a shovel full of earth out of the garden (failing this ashes or cinders will do as well), and throw them over the fat. Continue doing so till the blaze dies out, which it soon will do.

1080. **The Gentle Art of Driving a Tack.**—When putting a tack into a place where it is difficult to hold it with the fingers, thrust it through a piece of card or paper.

1081. **Green Stains on Stone.**—Where outdoor stonework is stained green, scour with hot water and soap. Rub on a little pipeclay and leave it on a few days. When washed off the stonework will be quite a normal colour.

1082.  **Mixing Mustard.**—Mustard mixed with salt and water keeps moist longer, and is more easily washed off when done with.  This is better than mixing with milk, because milk quickly sours.

1083.  **Keep a Vitamine Chart.**—Cut out from one of the ladies' papers or from a daily newspaper the list of vitamine A, B and C foods, now so much talked of and so essential to health.  Paste it on white cardboard and keep it handy for reference when planning the meals of the household. It is a great help, and the improved health of the family will amply repay you.

1084.  **Pickles—Don't Use Stone Jars.**—When making pickles use glass jars for storing, and not stone ones, on account of the acid in the vinegar, which dissolves any lead which may be present.

1085.  **Keeping Meat Good.**—To keep meat good in summer and to keep away the flies, dust well with pepper. An additional advantage is that the pepper is dry, and helps to conserve the meat juices.

1086.  **For Aspidistras.**—When a new leaf appears on an aspidistra plant, roll a piece of writing paper into a tube and place over it.  The leaf will then grow up quickly and straight as the light draws it up.

1087.  **When Making-up Beds to be Left Over the Holiday Period,** fold up the quilt and blankets, and pull the bottom half of the mattress over them.   Cover the whole with an old blanket, which will absorb all the moisture and leave the bed perfectly dry.

1088.  **To Fluff Up a Blanket.**—After a blanket has been washed and dried, peg it out on the line and beat with a carpet beater or old tennis racquet.  This makes it beautifully soft and fluffy.

1089. **To Clean a Boiler.**—To clean the inside of a boiler used for washing clothes, scour well with Glitto made into a paste with turpentine. Wash it off with hot water and preservene soap, and polish by rubbing well with a dry cloth.

1090. **Nettlerash.**—A quick and safe method of dealing with nettlerash is to rub the part affected with raw fresh parsley until it is quite green with the sap from it.

1091. **To Test Drain Pipes.**—Pour hot water mixed with oil of peppermint down the the drain to test it. If there is no leakage there will be no smell from the peppermint.

1092. **The Handy Trestle.**—A pair of trestles are a handy addition to the housewife's equipment. With these and a board a table can be set up in the kitchen for making pastry and cakes, for ironing, carving, cutting out, sewing, etc. This extra table can be added, if required, to the ordinary kitchen or dining room table or made into a side table or buffet for special occasions, if covered with a suitable cloth.

1093. **For a Tight Screw.** If a screw refuses to leave the wood in which it is embedded, place a screwdriver in the top of it, and give it a sharp tap with the hammer. This loosens the wood etc., adhering to it and the screw can be withdrawn easily.

1094. **For Light Pastry.**—Roll out your pastry with clean bottle on a sheet of glass, or a slab of marble, and it will be twice as light.

1095. **A Jelly Hint.**—When making jellies and blancmanges, add a little extra liquid in winter, otherwise they will be too stiff. In summer use a little less than the specified quantity, or they will not set well.

1096. **Soften Limy Water with Borax.**—If a thick scum of lime forms over the top of the water in the washing copper, the water is hard, and borax must be added each wash-day to dissolve the lime held in solution.

1097. **When Making Jellies** always stand the mould for a few minutes in cold water to ensure that the inside is wet all over ; the jelly will set quicker and turn out more easily.

1098. **To Re-Cover Deck Chairs.**—To re-cover a deck chair easily so that it will last, use double the usual length of canvas. Put it on without nailing ; exactly like a roller towel on a roller. It can then be moved along as one part gets worn or soiled.

1099. **To Prevent Juice from Boiling Over.**—To prevent juice from boiling over when making fruit pies or tarts, wet the edges with milk instead of water, as they then stick better.

1100. **For Ingrowing Nails.**—For an ingrowing toe-nail, get a pair of sharp scissors and make a V-shaped incision in the centre of the nail, which will then grow quite straight.

1101. **Lost Knobs on Drawers.**—If a knob comes off the kitchen drawer, screw on in its place an empty sewing cotton reel, and few people would notice the difference.

1102. **When Knitting Socks, etc.**—To estimate roughly the amount of wool required to knit a jumper or woollen coat, take a similar garment and weigh it. The same applies to socks.

1103. **For Cut Flowers.**—If a piece of charcoal is placed in water in which cut flowers are kept, they will keep fresh longer and the water will not smell unwholesome.

1104. **Ink Stains on Wood (To Remove).**—Ink stains can be got out of wooden floors or tables by using oxalic acid. Put it on with a brush.

1105. **To Stiffen Lace.**—If a lace collar is required in a hurry and there happens to be no starch made, dip it in a little milk. After ironing, it will come up just stiff enough.

1106. **Rat Paste.**—To destroy rats and mice, melt a pound of lard and stir into it half an ounce of phosphorus carefully. When nearly cold, thicken with flour and spread the paste on small pieces of brown paper. Lay them near the rat holes, when they will eat the paste greedily with fatal results.

1107. **To Sew On Buttons.**—To sew on a button so as to withstand wear and tear, let the stitches be fairly loose. Finish off by wrapping the sewing-cotton round and round under the button, so as to form a stalk. It will then be easier to push through the button-hole, and will keep on longer.

1108. **Hands, To protect when handling Coal.**—Keep an old glove in the coal house for slipping on the right hand when filling the coal bucket. Keep another in the coal vase for use when coaling the fire. These can be made with a thumb but no fingers, like a baby's glove. Cut out in any old cloth or odd material left over and stitch up with the sewing machine.

1109. **To Replace an Airing Cupboard.**—Where there is no airing cupboard in connection with the hot water system of the house, place a hot water bottle in the linen cupboard to keep the things well aired.

1110.  **For Hot and Perspiring Hands or Feet.**—If the hands perspire freely and are uncomfortably hot, dust them well with boracic powder when putting on the gloves to go out for the evening.  This will keep them both cool and dry.  For the feet, merely shake a little in the shoes.

1111.  **When Short of Butter.**—If there is very little butter in the house and it is wanted in a hurry, add a little milk to what you already have, and it will go twice as far if well beaten up.

1112.  **Care of Dishcloths.**—An easy way to ensure a clean, wholesome dishcloth is to keep two going at once. Peg one out on the line to dry and sweeten while the other is in use.

1113.  **Tarnish from Silver.**—Tarnish can be removed from silver and the silver thoroughly cleaned by soaking it in a bowl of hot water, a tiny bit of soda and a little Polivit a shiny metal sheet sold by all ironmongers.  Rinse, and wipe dry only.

1114.  **For Cutting-out.**—When cutting-out use a double tracing wheel, which gives a line for cutting to and a line to stitch on, thus saving both time and worry.

1115.  **Bread Crumbs.**—Always keep prepared bread crumbs by you in a tightly corked bottle.  They are invaluable for many dishes and it saves time to keep them ready.  Brown stale bread in the oven, then grate to form the crumbs.  They will keep a long time in a dry place.

1116.  **For the Amateur Milliner.**—When trimming hats always make large stitches on the wrong side and tiny ones on the right.  This is done in the trade, and it lessens the work considerably.

IDEAS FOR THE HOME

1117. **First-Aid in the Home.**—A small bottle of iodine and brush for applying it saves lots of worry. Use it for every cut and scratch as soon as discovered, and there will be no ill-effects afterwards.

1118. **When Folding Over Pastry** to make Cornish pasties, or Eccles cakes, always wet with brush first, and the edges will stick together firmly.

1119. **For Overdone Cakes.**—If cakes or bread happen to be overdone, wrap while warm in a nice clean cloth and leave half an hour. This steams and softens the hard crust and renders it more palatable.

1120. **To Cook Onions Quickly.**—When cooked onions are required in a hurry, a handy way is to peel them, then grate them finely on a grater. If wanted for a stew, pie, or for onion sauce, they will then cook in half the time.

1121. **When Boiling a Pudding,** cover the top with a buttered paper, tie this securely, leaving a piece of string long enough to cross the top of the basin loosely, and to tie on the opposite side. This forms a handle, and will save much time and trouble when lifting the pudding from the pan in which it is boiled.

1122. **Cooking Hint.**—Always let a cake or pudding stand five minutes before turning it out, so as to allow it to shrink a little.

1123. **Pancake Hint.**—A tablespoonful of melted butter added to pancake batter just before frying will improve the colour and they will not stick to the pan.

1124. **To Make Melons or Grape Fruit Icy Cold Without Ice.**—Put them in a pail of water in the sink and leave the tap just dripping overnight.

**1125. Table Etiquette and Hints.**—When consuming soup tilt the plate away from you and ladle the soup out of the plate away from you as well. To open a boiled egg tap it round with the spoon and neatly scoop off the top. Take an olive or a salted almond up in your fingers just as you would a chocolate. A dry white wine means merely "not sweet." Sherry is correct with the soup only. Claret with the meat. Port with the walnuts. Prairie Oyster is a concoction that is supposed to take away the effects of "the morning after the night before." It is made of a raw egg, whisky, and Worcester sauce. About tips : don't over-do it. If well looked after about ten per cent. of the bill is quite enough.

**1126. A Handy Screen.**—A small clothes horse may be made into a screen with pretty cretonnne, and fitted with bags, hooks, pockets and elastic bands, and is a most useful possession to an invalid.

**1127. Cooking Hint.**—If meat, puddings, tarts and cakes are always covered with butter-paper nothing will be burnt black in the oven.

**1128. In the Nursery.**—When reading stories to children insert their own names for those in the story, it will interest them and keep their attention.

**1129. A Warm Eiderdown.**—Save all the old blankets and tack the best parts together, say a couple of thicknesses. Then cover with cretonne and machine stitch across, about four inches apart. A nice eiderdown is thus made at little cost. The colour scheme of cretonne should be in harmony with other covers in bedroom.

**1130. A Glass Hint.**—When you buy new glasses, put them in a pan of cold water and place over a slow fire until the water reaches the boiling point. Take from the fire and let cool in the water. Be sure the glasses are thoroughly covered with water while on the fire. Ice-water or hot fluids will not affect the tempered glasses.

1131. **To Clean Playing Cards.**—Place them on a news-paper or tray, sprinkle with talcum powder, and rub with a piece of clean, dry cheese-cloth, or other soft dry cloth.

1132. **To Clean Kitchen Tables and Shelves.**—Take half-pound of sand and half-pound of lime. Work dissolved preservene soap into the dry ingredients. Put the mixture on with a scrubbing brush, and wash off with plenty of cold water. This mixture proves an excellent cleanser and it preserves the wood.

1133. **To Remove Grease from Tables.**—Lemon juice well rubbed into kitchen tables quickly removes all grease.

1134. **Potato Liquid Removes Coffee and Tea Stains.**—The water in which potatoes have been boiled will remove tea and coffee stains from napkins and tablecloths if they are soaked in it before washing.

1135. **To Take Dents Out of Wood.**—First put a wet cloth over the dent and then place a hot iron on the cloth. Repeat until the dent has disappeared.

1136. **A Bath Hint.**—The risk of slipping in the bath causes much anxiety to elderly or infirm people. This can be obviated by placing in the bath a rubber composition mat. This mat has a slightly corrugated surface.

1137. **Sea Water Stains.**—Sea water makes extremely ugly marks on brown shoes. The only really effective way of removing them is to dissolve a small lump of ordinary washing soda in two tablespoonfuls of hot milk and dab it round the stains. Allow it to thoroughly dry, which does not take many minutes, then repeat the process When the second coat has dried on, clean the shoes with ordinary polish. No stains will then be visible.

1138. **A Seashore Hint.**—When going to the sea it should be remembered that sea water quickly rots the stitches in boots. A copper or two spent on oak copal varnish, which should be painted in between the soles and uppers, is thus money well spent.

1139. **Sea water Marks on Black Boots.**—If sea water makes white marks on black boots, the easiest remedy is to rub the marks with a paste made of black lead and lemon juice. Leave for an hour and then allow to dry off.

1140. **To Protect Furs.**—Sprinkle furs with black pepper and lay away in the dark, and moths will not touch them. This does not smell as badly as moth balls.

1141. **To Lengthen a Dress.**—A good way of lengthening a dress without showing is put an inch tuck nearly at the bottom of the dress before you turn the hem up. The tuck will not show, as it will be in the hem. To lengthen you simply undo the tuck.

1142. **How to Stain a Floor.**—Go over the floor with pincers, removing old nails, and then scrub well. Paint marks must also be scratched away with the help of turpentine, the staining of the floor is a matter of taste. A deep and lasting stain can be produced by the use of either Solignum or permanganate of potash. Should you decide on the latter, buy half a pound of the cheapest variety, melt down with hot water in about three-quarters of a pail full of water. Then apply with a mop or paint brush, which should be a cheap one, for the brush will be spoilt. This amount of permanganate will stain a fair-sized floor. A cheap stain is made with Vandyke Brown pigment from the oilshop, mixed with ammonia and water. To make, mix Vandyke Brown and ammonia and add water to make it the right hue. All stains which are without varnish need either to be polished or varnished to finish the effect. Should varnish be used, wash the already brown stained floor over with size, to prevent varnish sinking in unduly, and this will prove an economy. The floor must be quite dry before applying varnish, using straight and even strokes of the brush. A very nice polish can be obtained by using beeswax and turpentine. A polishing pad with a handle saves a great deal of exertion, as it is pushed over the floor and polishes by its weight. A most economical almost black stain is made by mixing a tin of japan black, such as is used for painting iron work, with methylated spirit to the desired colour. This produces a varnish stain, so there is not so much trouble with polishing afterwards.

1143. **Paper Fire-lighters.**—Put old newspapers into a pail of water and let them soak for several days. Then tear up the pulp, and squeeze into hard balls. Put them in a warm place to dry. They will be found excellent for lighting fires, or keeping them alight. They also make excellent fuel for the copper fire.

1144. **To Clean Oilcloth.**—Rub oilcloth with a rag dipped in skim milk and polish with a dry soft cloth. This method gives a wonderful polish and preserves the oilcloth, as washing with soap and water is not necessary.

1145. **To Clean Cloth Gaiters and Leggings.**—For cleaning light coloured or drab gaiters, peel and grate a few potatoes and pass them through a mincing machine into a basin. Sponge the cloth thoroughly all over with the pulp. Hang gaiters up to dry, then well brush. This method will make the cloth look like new.

1146. **To soften water** shred some preservene soap and put into a pan with a little cold water. Heat this until dissolved, and then add a small lump of soda. Bottle till wanted for use.

1147.  **Care of the Hair.**—To prevent falling hair rub well into the scalp with equal parts of lemon juice and glycerine. This is an excellent remedy for dandruff. Hair should be thoroughly brushed for ten minutes night and morning to retain a natural glossy sheen.

1148.  **Boiling Clothes in Copper.**—Have a good-sized piece of galvanised zinc perforated and bent so that it fits well into the bottom of the copper. When the water is brought to the boil it forces its way up through the holes and thus doubles the action of the boiling.

1149.  **Casement Curtains and Valance : To Fit Without Valance Board.** Buy ordinary iron brackets about four inches in depth and fix these at either end of your window and at any angles which occur. To these can be fixed, quite close to the window frame, either wood or brass rods, brass preferably, because they do not sag. The rods should be quite thin and rings bought large enough to slip over easily. Curtain pins of the new pattern are best to buy. Fasten these at short intervals to the top of the curtain, but do not gather the curtain at all. Then put the curtains up. Now comes the valance. Get ordinary springs such as men use for keeping their shirt sleeves up. One spring for each curtain. Cut them in the centre so that they lie quite flat. Attach a tape to each end so that the whole is about the length of the valance. Then make the valance with a good deep heading at the top and allow a hem wide enough to take the spring easily. Run the spring and tape through the valance and fasten the ends of the tape to the iron brackets. You will find that the spring in the centre of the hem will hold the curtain quite taut and it will not sag like curtains which are hung on tape. The effect is the same as if the valance were fastened to a board. The curtains not being gathered or pleated, they can be pulled across the window quite easily in the evenings, and thus provide effective blinds.

1150. **A Pickling Hint.**—Add a little beetroot to red cabbage when pickling. It will then be a richer colour.

1151. **Pickled Cabbage.**—Never use a stale cabbage for pickling, as the pickle will be flabby when done.

1152. **Ginger Snaps.**—To curl ginger or "brandy" snaps after they are baked, roll them round the handle of a spoon.

1153. **Parcels Post Box**—For the purpose of the household's parcel packing, keep a large stout cardboard box, known to the family as the "Parcels Box" and always kept in the same place when not actually in use. In it would be kept: (1) a ball of string; (2) odd pieces of string, various thicknesses; (3) sealing wax; (4) luggage tags; (5) luggage labels; (6) gum; (7) fine cord; (8) chart of parcels post rates.

1154. **That Extra Table.**—When an extra table is required for cutting-out, or any other purpose, it can easily be improvised by keeping in the house a spare board. Place one end on the table and the other on the sideboard, a Chesterfield, or a chair-back, and there it is.

1155. **Tan Shoes.**—If black shoes are desired in place of tan, one or two applications of black boot polish will stain them quite effectually, and be permanent as well.

1156. **When Preserving Plums.**—When preserving plums or damsons, prick the ends with a silver fork.

1157. **When Making Marmalade.**—When making orange or lemon marmalade, put the pips in a small muslin bag and boil with the fruit. This helps the marmalade to set better.

1158. **To Prevent Burst Pipes.**—When leaving the house in winter, let the taps drip gently while away, as this prevents the water from freezing. There will then be no burst pipes on your return.

1159.  **To Draw a Fowl.**—To draw a fowl, lay it on a board and keep handy a basin of common salt.  Damp the hands and dip in the latter, when a better grip can be obtained and the work becomes easy.

1160.  **How to Pour Pepper.**—When putting pepper in the cruet, the easiest way is to let it run through a small hole cut in the corner of an envelope.  Nothing is spilt and much time is saved.

1161.  **An Improvised Hat Box.**—To keep hats free from dust and handy to get at, get a large cardboard Post Toastie box from the grocer and cover it with cretonne.  It will hold several, and the four-fold lid keeps them dust-proof.

1162.  **As a Dark Staircase** is sometimes dangerous as well as unsightly, arrange a mirror somewhere at an angle so as to catch and reflect light.  Have a bright carpet and where possible white or light paintwork.

1163.  **An Easily-made Pram Cover.**—Take a piece of old blanket and cut it to the required size.  Dye it any pretty shade desired, then buttonhole the edges with wool of a contrasting shade.  Work an initial in the middle with the same coloured wool, and you will have an easily-made, attractive cover.

1164.  **Flour Browning.**—When browning flour during cooking operations, do not apply too much heat, as that makes it bitter.

1165.  **To Purify the Air.**  To purify the air in a room, burn some coffee on a hot shovel placed on a brick in the middle of the room.  Keep the room closed for a few minutes.  When re-opened it will have a delightfully refreshing odour.  Buy only the cheapest coffee for this purpose.

1166. **For Hot Hands.**—When doing fine sewing or knitting in hot weather and the hands get moist, dip them frequently in powdered French chalk.

1167. **When Dry Cleaning** anything with petrol, always use a second bath of petrol for rinsing. The operation is called dry cleaning because no water is used.

1168. **Shopping Basket.**—Give your shopping basket a cleanse occasionally and it will be more cleanly and hygienic for carrying foods. Dip in hot soapsuds made with preservene soap. The latter will penetrate into all the interstices and fetch out the dirt without injuring the basketwork. It does it while you watch.

1169. **Before Spring Cleaning.**—Before commencing spring cleaning operations, go through the house and take stock of all brass bedsteads, fireirons, fenders, etc. which have become shabby, and send them away to be re-lacquered. Not only will they be out of the way during the annual upheaval, but they will be much better fitted to take their place in the scheme of things when everything gets back to its own place again.

1170. **Wet Wash Day.**—If it happens to be wet on the wash-day, try drying the clothes in the airing cupboard. With a little ingenuity it can be done. Have two wooden trays made like large grids and fit them on to the sides of the wall. Lay the clothes on these and keep turning them. A little extra fire in the kitchen will be required to keep the airing cupboard warm.

1171. **When Buying Meat.**—When choosing a joint, always remember that good meat has a marbled appearance and is of a medium colour, i.e., neither pale nor too red.

1172. **Tannin-less Tea.**—To prevent excess of tannin in tea, pour it into a second clean teapot three minutes after it has been mashed. It is allowing the tea to stand on the leaves which causes an excess of tannin.

1173. **Use Onion Powder.**—If an onion flavour is required for a dish and there is no time to cook a fresh onion, add a pinch of onion powder. This imparts the requisite flavour and keeps for months if placed in an airtight tin.

1174. **To Procure Clean Milk.**—After milk has stood for some time in a jug, pour it into another vessel carefully, when a sediment will be seen at the bottom. Leave this, as it consists of impurities collected from the atmosphere and elsewhere.

1175. **Gingerbread.**—When making gingerbread, warm the treacle before mixing it in. This makes it run better, and makes the cake lighter. The same rule applies to ginger puddings.

1176. **A Stocking Hint.**—Sew a piece of wide tape round the tops of stockings. This will prevent the possibility of suspenders tearing them and thus prolong their life.

1177. **For Squeaky Shoes.**—If your new shoes squeak when walking, dip a rag in boiled linseed oil and rub the soles all over. One or two applications will quite eradicate the squeak.

1178. **Transfers.**—When one pattern has been taken from tracing paper with a hot iron, go over the faint lines with a thick blue lead such as packers use. Another impression can then be obtained, and the pattern used repeatedly in this way.

1179. **For a Beaded Lamp Shade.**—A beaded lamp shade can be made beautifully clean by using preservene soap. Make a nice hot lather in a wide bowl or bucket, shake the shade free from dust and immerse. Move quickly up and down until the dirty drops out, rinse in two waters, drain, and fasten to clothes line in the open air to dry.

1180. **Ironing Stiff Collars.**—When ironing a gent's or boy's collar, curl it upwards with the left hand, while holding the iron in the right. A sharp pull or two will cause the front edges to almost meet.

1181. **To Prevent Ink Stains.**—When the children are doing home-lessons in the evenings, or any odd writing, safeguard the tablecloth by insisting on the inkstand or bottle being placed on a large sheet of stout cardboard, or a large flat dish. Even if ink should then be spilt it can do little or no harm.

1182. **To Take Up Ladders.**—A ladder in a silk stocking when ready to go out is little short of a calamity. To remedy the defect take a fine crochet hook, lift up the stitch, and pull the strands through till you reach the top, when the stocking will appear as usual.

1183. **A Badly Creased Dress.**—If a dress or costume has been packed badly and is sent home creased and unfit to wear, do not iron it, or press in any way, as by so doing you take off the " new " look. Hang it by the fire for an hour or two, and the creases will drop out of themselves.

1184. **When Using Waving Irons.**—When using curling tongs or waving irons, always place a piece of soft paper between the hair and the tongs. This prevents scorching and discolouration. Too hot irons in contact with the hair tend to darken it if light.

1185.  **For Rheumatism.**—If you are troubled with rheumatism, drink plenty of lemon juice, eat celery, and drink the water in which celery has been boiled.

1186.  **To Destroy Beetles.**—Make some plaster of paris into a paste with lard and spread on pieces of brown paper. This will effectively destroy beetles and cockroaches.

1187.  **Draining Boards.**—A fixed draining board placed on each side of the kitchen sink saves hours of labour, as does a plate rack fixed near the sink on the wall.

1188.  **Rheumatism.**—A simple and effective way to ease rheumatic pains is to bathe the parts with water in which potatoes have been boiled.  A daily bathe with this potato water is excellent.

1189.  **How to Treat Aspidistras.**—These plants will keep and look healthy if properly treated and given a good sponging once a fortnight.  Place the plant in a bucket of clean cold water, the latter to come just over the rim of the plant-pot.  Take a bowl of warm water, dip into it a soft piece of flannel and soap it well with soap.  Rub every leaf all over, the under sides as well.  Rinse the flannel well and do the leaves again, removing as much of the soap as possible.  Spray with clean water from a watering can and the plant will need no further attention for a fortnight. The soap gives a beautiful gloss to the leaves as well.

1190.  **A Cake Hint.**—Use sour milk if you want a light cake, it is much better than fresh milk.  Sweet milk makes cake cut like pound cake.

1191.  **A Brush Rack.**—A handy article for kitchen use is a rack on which can be hung all the brushes and mops used during cleaning operations.  This keeps them together and much running about is saved.

1192.  **When Boiling Potatoes,** pour off the first water as soon as it boils, refill the saucepan, and the potatoes will boil quite white.

1193.  **Ironing Hint.**—To avoid making creases when ironing and to obviate the necessary re-ironing when this occurs, the housewife should make it a rule always to iron away from herself, keeping the unironed portion nearest her.

1194.  **For Cooling Cakes.**—A shallow wire letter basket, if turned upside down, makes an excellent cooling tray for home-made cakes, pastry, biscuits, etc.

1195.  **For the Pantry.**—To keep the pantry clean and sweet-smelling, remove all crumbs, crusts, and odd bits of left-over food every morning.

1196.  **Use Water for Omelettes.**—When making omelettes, or when making the batter for Yorkshire puddings and pancakes, remember that half a cupful of cold water added to the milk will make them considerably lighter than if mixed with milk only.

1197.  **Gravy.**—To test if gravy is of the right consistency see if it flows over the dish like thick cream.  If so, it is just right.

1198.  **To Spray a Sickroom.**—To remove the somewhat sickly odour which sometimes clings to a sickroom, the air should be sprayed occasionally. An efficient spray, such as is used for spraying plants, can be purchased from a seedsman for a few coppers.  Any perfume or disinfectant can be sprayed through it, without coming in contact with the user's mouth, the operation being at once quick and effective.

1199. **Useful Set of Patterns.**—Patterns of under-garments for every member of the household, if kept handy together in a box, save lots of work and labour. As the children grow bigger they can be slightly altered, while for adult members they can be utilised year after year with very little alteration indeed.

1200. **Document Box.**—The housewife can save herself much work and worry by keeping all her important papers, accounts, etc, in a locked box bought for the purpose.

1201. **For Useful Recipes.**—A Housewife's Cutting Book is a great convenience in the home. Get a news-paper cutting book from the stationer, and paste in under different headings good cookery recipes and any household and health hints that you come across and are interested in. Make an index and the book, when finished, will contain just the information particularly suited to the needs of your household.

1202. **Odd Button Box.**—Always keep a tin or box for odd buttons of all kinds and sizes. Drop them in as they come along and you will usually find just the thing you want when a button has to be hurriedly produced and sewn on.

1203. **The Egg-timer.**—Have your egg-timer mounted on a strip of wood with a hole bored in the top. Hang it up near the cooking stove, and you will save yourself much worry.

1204. **For a Leaky Washtub.**—If a wooden washtub or trough leaks, it is due to the dryness and consequent shrinkage of the wood. To remedy this, put it out of doors on a wet day, and fill it with tap water. This causes the wood to swell, and the leak disappears.

1205. **To Bake a Fruit Tart.**—Use plenty of heat at first to bake the pastry quickly, then turn down the gas and cook slowly to ensure the fruit being done sufficiently.

1206. **A Neck Bleach.**—As the neck easily gets discoloured, a good bleach can be made by taking equal parts of glycerine and lemon-juice and mixing together. Add a few drops of any desired perfume and apply the bleach at night before retiring. Wash off with warm water next morning, and if this is repeated two or three times the neck will become quite white.

1207. **A Hand Bath Spray.**—Procure a piece of piping from your ironmonger and have a nozzle and rose fixed at one end. Attach the other end to the bath tap and you can find an excellent and invigorating " shower " with very little trouble.

1208. **Perfumed Paper Handkerchiefs.**—Paper handkerchiefs, perfumed and medicated, would be of immense advantage to persons suffering from a cold in the head. They could be burnt as soon as done with.

1209. **To Fry Potatoes.**—When frying potatoes, etc., do not put in too many at once as this lowers the temperature of the fat.

1210. **Success in Pastry-making.**—Success in making pastry depends on keeping everything as cool as possible, but place the pastry in a very hot oven as soon as made.

1211. **To Trap Ants.**—If ants get into a pantry or cupboard, leave an empty honey jar there—unwashed. They will cluster round the little honey remaining and can easily be caught and destroyed.

1212.  **Damp Beds.**—To test whether a bed is damp or not, put a handmirror between the sheets.  If damp, the glass will be misty.  A watch answers the same purpose, as the damp will show on the glass covering the face in a few seconds.

1213.  **When Buying a Toothbrush.**—When buying a toothbrush, it pays to give a little more and get a good quality article, as inferior brushes often shed their bristles, and these when swallowed have been known to set up appendicitis and other troubles.

1214.  **To Clean Herrings.**—When cooking herrings be careful to remove the silver gut (which appears as a long strip of silvery lining) and remove the backbone by slipping the thumb under to loosen it.

1215.  **A Hot Salt Bag.**—For toothache, ear ache and other minor aches and pains a cure can often be effected and a good night's rest be secured by the aid of a hot salt bag.  This can be made from an oblong piece of calico folded across the centre and machine stitched along three edges.  Heat some salt over the gas or fire, fill the bag and sew it up.  Place the hot bag on the affected part, when relief will be obtained almost immediately.  The efficacy of this treatment lies in the fact that salt, when heated, retains the heat for a long time.

1216.  **A Table Bedstead.**—I suggest that the space underneath a dining-room table be made so that it would hold a mattress.  The top could be made to open by turning a screw, as at present when an extra leaf is put in, and the top slide away in two halves.  This would give an extra bed when more accommodation is required occasionally.

1217. **Airing a Bed.**—When using a hot-water bottle to air or warm a bed, do not place it flat, but stand it on one end. This makes a hot air chamber, and the heat gets all over instead of being concentrated on one spot.

1218. **Steaming.**—If there is no steamer to hand, vegetables can be steamed by placing in a colander over a saucepan of boiling water. Steaming always requires a longer time than boiling.

1219. **For Burnt Cakes.**—For burnt cakes or bread, rub while still hot with a nutmeg grater. This quickly removes the burnt crust.

1220. **Aspidistras.**—If your aspidistra looks sick, push a rusty nail in the soil and keep it well watered. The iron in the nail helps to feed the soil.

1221. **For Roses.**—Give your roses lime in the form of broken egg shells and they will quickly repay you for your trouble. Cover the broken shell with a layer of soil.

1222. **A Handy Fire Extinguisher.**—A good thing to have in the house at all times would be a fire extinguisher in powder form. A little could be used for a chimney accidentally set on fire, etc.

1223. **To Renovate a Man's Hat.**—Remove the hat band and brush the hat thoroughly well. Wipe over with a rag dipped in petrol, but do this out of doors, as petrol vapour is very inflammable. Wash the hat band in preservene soap lather, using two different lots of water. Rinse, wring, iron on wrong side, and stitch on to hat again, thus giving it a new lease of life.

1224. **To Boil Salt Meat.**—Salt meat is easy to cook put into cold water first and gradually brought to the boil after which it should simmer slowly.

1225.  **The Breakfast Bacon.**—The breakfast bacon will be much easier to cut if the rind is stripped off all in one piece.  The rashers can then be made of any desired thickness.

1226.  **Home-made Tooth Paste.**—An excellent tooth paste can be easily made at home by mixing together equal portions of powdered camphor and precipitated chalk.

1227.  **Lace Edgings in the Wash.**—All lace edgings and narrow apron and other strings should be pulled out straight and flat, when being pegged out on the line, as they are then twice as easy to iron.

1228.  **Millinery Hint.**—Have two sets of trimming for your hat it you like variety.  Each set should be fitted with press-studs corresponding to similar press-studs on the shape.  Two or three minutes will suffice to remove one trimming and put on the other.

1229.  **For Pastry Cutting.**—If the pastry-cutter is lost or mislaid, use the rim of a tumbler instead for cutting out the rounds.

1230.  **To Cook Sausages.**—When cooking sausages, dip each one in milk, roll in flour, and plunge into hot fat from which a blue smoke is rising.   Done in this way, they will not split.

1231.  **For Shirt Buttons.**—When making shirts at home instead of stitching the buttons on the shirt, stitch them on a narrow piece of shirting at distances to correspond with the button-holes.  Fasten in position with a tiny safety pin at the top and bottom.  They can then easily be removed when wash-day comes round and there will be no more broken buttons.

1232.  **To Clean Leather Goods.**—Nothing can beat petrol for cleaning all kinds of fancy leather goods—hats, bags, cushions, etc.  Put it on with a brush, but do it out of doors, as petrol is very inflammable.  Rinse and polish afterwards with a soft cloth.

1233.  **For Yorkshire Puddings.**—If the batter is mixed an hour or two before it is required, it will be lighter and require less beating.

1234.  **Knitting Hint.**—When knitting the front of a jumper and the stitches have to be halved, there is no need to take one half off the needle.  Leave them on, and knit with the other end of the same needle.

1235.  **Patching.**—When it is necessary to put on a patch do so with the sewing machine.  Besides being done in a quarter of the time, the machine flattens the material and holds it firmly in position.  Even blankets can be patched with the sewing machine in this way, if the patches are first tacked on loosely.

1236.  **For the Workbasket.**—A tiny packet in one corner of the workbasket should always contain a thimble.  This saves much worry and loss of time searching for one.

1237.  **Draught Excluder.**—Tack strips of an old felt hat along the bottom and sides of the door.  This will block out all draught and make the room quite comfortable.

1238.  **To Make a Salad.**—To make a successful salad, dry the green vegetables (after washing) in a clean towel and break them up instead of cutting them.

1239.  **An Envelope Box.**—An envelope box is a real time saver, and it saves much worry too.  Any kind of box will suffice and in it should be placed all kinds and sizes of envelopes, including one or two registered envelopes, for use in an emergency, and a few large square ones.

1240.　**To Polish New Boots.**—If new boots do not polish readily, rub them with the cut half of a fresh lemon. Let it dry on, then polish up in the usual way.

1241.　**For Home Dyeing.**—To get a beige or old ivory shade when dyeing gloves, stockings or lace, put a little cold tea in the water. The dye will be quite permanent and can be used for dyeing silk or cotton for darning purposes.

1242.　**For the Windows.**—For opening windows which are large and lofty, such as bedroom windows in old houses, the housewife should keep by her a hooked stick long enough to reach the eyelet hole in the top of the window-frame. The window can then easily be pulled down to open it for airing the room. For closing, use the other end of the pole and push the top window frame up.

1243.　**For Casserole Cookery**—Casserole cookery is best done over a low gas ring, placing the casserole on an asbestos mat. For washday dinners this method of cookery is ideal, making delicious stews and soups with a minimum of trouble.

1244.　**For Earache.**—One of the best and safest ways of relieving this is to slightly warm a little castor oil and apply it to the ear nearest where the pain is.

1245.　**Grease Marks.**—Grease marks can be removed from the most delicate material if French chalk is sprinkled thickly over it on the wrong side. Leave the chalk on until it has absorbed all the grease. Then shake off, and press gently on the wrong side with a warm, but not with a hot iron.

1246.　**For Bathroom Use.**—Always keep an odd glass jam jar in the bathroom as a receptacle for the spent matches used by the family when lighting the gas, especially in winter. Besides saving the labour of collecting them from odd corners and clearing away, this method is far safer.

1247. **A New Gas Globe.**—Instead of using a glass globe buy one of the new wire globes now on the market. Besides being washable, they are unbreakable, and save many a journey for a new globe when one gets broken in the kitchen.

1248. **An Effective Door-stop.**—If a door bangs against a wall each time it is opened and destroys the plaster, place a round rubber doorstop at the back of it and in front of the wall.

1249. **Damp Salt.**—To prevent salt turning damp in the cupboard or even in the cruet, place it on a clean sheet of paper to dry as soon as it is purchased. When thoroughly dry, mix with it a little cornflour and you will not again be troubled with damp salt.

1250. **To Store Onions.**—To prevent onions growing when storing, singe the roots thoroughly with a red hot poker. Always hang up onions in a dark cool place when storing, and use them as required, leaving the bulk to hang.

1251. **A Quickly-made Hat.**—Purchase a buckram shape. Paint it with Indian ink, using a large brush. Take care not to let it dry in patches. The ink is waterproof and will never run. Fasten a plume or other ornament in front and the hat is ready for wear.

1252. **Castors.**—Castors should be oiled occasionally as less strength is then required to pull the furniture about for cleaning.

1253. **Substitute for Fish Kettle.**—When boiling fish without a fish kettle, use a plate and cheesecloth with the corners knotted. Place the cheesecloth under the plate and when the fish is done, lift out by the knotted corners and drain well before serving.

1254. **A Medicine Chest.**—This is a real time-saver in an emergency. If a cupboard is not available, use a fair-sized wooden box with a lid. But always keep it in the same place and out of the way of children. Let every member of the household know where it is kept. In it place bandages, court plaster, castor oil, sal volatile, ointments, tincture of iodine, etc.

1255. **Sour Milk.**—Sour Milk makes lighter cakes, puddings, scones and omelettes. It can also be used for polishing lacquered trays which should never have water near them.

1256. **Before Removing,** get all carpets cut ready to fit the new floors, and new ones ready where necessary, this greatly shortens the process of getting "settled" down again.

1257. **To Beat Butter and Sugar.**—Where a recipe requires the beating of butter and sugar to a cream, much arm ache can be saved by placing these ingredients in a basin over a kettle of hot water until partly blended. Then beat up as required.

1258. **A Carrier Bag.**—Always have a folded paper carrier in your handbag, as it often comes in useful for getting unexpected shopping parcels home.

1259. **Use of Soda.**—Never use soda in any form for washing silk or woollen articles. Soda is an alkali and not only turns these articles yellow, but tends to destroy the fibre as well.

1260. **When Cooking Cauliflower.**—Always cook cauliflower in an enamel lined saucepan and add a table-spoonful of vinegar to the water in which it is boiled. This gives it a nice white appearance.

1261. **Place for Piano.**—A piano will give out a better volume of sound if placed away from the wall, either entirely or at one end.

1262. **For Puddings.**—A boiled pudding should be plunged into boiling water and not simply hot; when a pudding is to be steamed the water over which it is placed must also be quite boiling to begin with. This makes the puddings lighter.

1263. **Decoration for Trifles.**—An easy and effective method of decorating a trifle is to scatter the small sweets known as " Hundreds and Thousands " over the top.

1264. **Herbs.**—Keep a bottle of dried mixed herbs in the kitchen cupboard. They are invaluable for flavourings.

1265. **Cupboard Fasteners.**—A good idea for cupboard fasteners is one which closes automatically (by catching when shut) and opens by pressing a knob. This contrivance would be less unsightly and more convenient.

1266. **A Net for Basins.**—Keep a beaded net handy, not only for milkjugs, but to cover sauces, custards, etc., in basins, especially in summer.

1267. **Lid Rack.**—Any home carpenter can make a serviceable but simple lid rack, consisting of a wooden framework with two or three staves across it. All the saucepan lids can rest on the staves, be always easily found when wanted, and dry off quicker after the washing-up is done.

1268. **For the Dressing Table Top.**—A lot of washing can be saved by having a sheet of plate glass on the top of the dressing table. Put a pretty duchesse cover underneath. It will show through the glass and last clean a long time.

1269. **To Decorate a Hem.**—When turning up a hem on an underskirt, try turning it up on the right side instead of the wrong side. Run it along—using large stitches—with filoselle or some other fancy silk or cotton. The hem will not only be quickly finished, but decorative as well.

1270. **To Make White Shoes Black.**—To render soiled white shoes quite black, paint lightly with black Indian Ink, as it is permanent and waterproof. Use a large brush and paint evenly.

1271. **Fire, to light quickly.**—Save and dry all orange and lemon peel, nut and cocoanut shells. They are ideal for lighting or livening up a fire, especially in a sick room, as they do not crackle like wood.

1272. **A Hinged Table.**—Where kitchen space is limited it is an excellent plan to fasten a board on to the window-sill (or to the wall under the sill) with a couple of hinges. When not required this can hang flat against the wall and takes up no room. When required, it can be used for cutting bread on, and for dozens of other household purposes where an extra table is an advantage.

1273. **For Stitching Ninon and Crêpe de Chine.**—When machine-stitching ninon and crêpe de chine, place thin white tissue paper underneath and remove after stitching.

1274. **Rubber Bands.**—Keep a few rubber bands in the house, as they have dozens of uses and save labour and trouble.

1275. **Dust Sheets.**—Always use a dust sheet when cleaning, as it saves hours of labour afterwards.

1276. **When Removing.**—Before removing, pack up the articles contained in each drawer and make a newspaper parcel of them. It is safer and much more convenient when re-arranging afterwards.

1277. **Line Your Rugs.**—To prevent the dirt from slipping through the kitchen rugs on to the floor, it is best to line the rugs with hessian or some cheap coarse material. The dirt can then all be removed at one operation.

1278. **A Boot Rack.**—Boots and shoes left in odd corners about the house make a lot of work for the house-wife when tidying up time comes. By making a couple of light frames similar to picture frames, and placing them crosswise, a light, portable boot and shoe rack is obtained, which saves many unnecessary steps.

1279. **Care of Umbrellas.**—Always turn an umbrella upside down to drain and the drippings will be all in one place, besides making the umbrella wear longer.

1280. **To Exterminate Earwigs.**—If earwigs are trouble-some in the house, saturate a sheet of blotting paper with oil of pennyroyal, obtainable for a few coppers from the chemist. Cut or tear the blotting paper into small pieces and lay it about the shelves in cupboard and pantry, when the earwigs will soon disappear.

1281. **A Blocked Sink Pipe.**—To clear a blocked sink pipe get some chloride of lime from the chemist. Stuff it into the pipe as tightly as possible, until it will hold no more. Pour in boiling water, slowly at first. The dissolv-ing chloride of lime will then burn out the obstructing rubbish and the way will be cleared.

1282. **First Aid. A Wet Day Hint.**—If soaked through, the best safeguard from future trouble is to get an immediate change into dry clothing, soak the feet in hot water containing mustard, and have a hot lemon drink. This is a marvellous preventive of dangerous colds.

1283. **Stair Rods.**—Old, discarded brass stair rods can be painted yellow and used for attic stairs. No cleaning is required except an occasional dust.

1284.  **Loaves of Bread** may be kept fresh for ten days if they are wrapped separately in grease-proof paper and placed on any airy shelf.

1285.  **Meat to be Eaten Cold** should not be cut when hot or there will be a great loss of valuable juices.

1286.  **Capers** are expensive to buy and so the economical housewife will pickle nasturtium seeds in good vinegar and so save her pocket.

1287.  **To Keep Cake Fresh,** put a piece of bread in the cake tin.

1288.  If you have any **stewed fruit left over** from lunch dissolve a jelly with the heated juice and pour the liquid over the fruit.  The result will be a very nice sweet for supper.

1289.  **Cold Potatoes left over from Dinner** make a very nice salad.  Slice them thinly, place on a glass dish with a boiled onion also sliced.  Cover with a little Mayonnaise sauce.

1290.  When **making pastry** remember to keep everything as cool as possible.  Work in a cool room away from the fire ; use cold water for mixing ; keep the hands cool and do as much of the work as possible with the tips of the fingers.  The flour must be perfectly dry and free from lumps.  Rolling should be done one way and never go off the edge of the pastry as if this is done all the air is forced out.

1291.  Do not make the **mixture of a fruit cake** too moist, or the fruit will all sink to the bottom.

1292.  **When Testing a Cake** to see if it be sufficiently cooked, always heat the knitting pin or skewer.

1293.  **Never Try to Dye an Article a Lighter Shade** than the original.

1294. **To Dye a Carpet,** clean thoroughly, prepare the dye according to the directions on the packet, using only half the quantity of water stated. Put on the dye with a soft pad of flannel.

1295. **To Clean Ribbons.**—Sponge gently with warm water and ammonia. Spread lengthwise on a table, cover with a thin cloth, and iron till dry.

1296. **To Revive a Shabby Silk Umbrella.**—Put a table-spoonful of sugar into a basin and pour over it half a pint of boiling water.

1297. **To Shrink Flannel.**—Before making up, soak for a night in cold water, then wring out of warm water in which a little soap has been dissolved.

1298. **Dry Cleaning at Home.**—Lay a penny lump of salt in the oven until warm. Well shake and brush the garment and lay on the table. Break off a piece of the salt and rub on the article till the salt is soiled. Continue till clean, then shake well and brush and place in the air or before the fire to take out creases.

1299. **If Lemon-juice is added to the Water when Boiling Rice** it will not only whiten it, but will separate the grains too.

1300. **Frozen Meat** should be thawed slowly by means of putting it into cold water and then wiping it dry with a cloth. It should then be hung up in the larder with the cut side uppermost, to prevent the juices from running out. Before you place it in the oven, turn the gas high for a few moments, the great heat will close the pores and thus keep the goodness in the meat. Lower the light and roast the meat very slowly in order to cook it through to the bone without wasting it.

1301. **Rub the Perambulator Hood** with a good boot polish once a week. It will prevent it cracking and improve its appearance.

1302.  **A Sausage Cooking Hint.**—To prevent sausages bursting, dip them in boiling water before placing in the frying pan or on the grill.

1303.  **A Quick Way to Make Raspings** is to place the dry crusts in a newspaper and put them through the mangle ; twice if necessary.   They crush much easier when hot.

1304.  **Dripping.**—When pouring fat into a basin, add one tablespoonful of boiling water.  This will make all pieces of meat sink to the bottom and the dripping will be nice and clear when set.

1305.  **Fried Eggs.**—To prevent fried eggs from breaking or sticking, add a teaspoonful of flour to the frying fat.

1306.  **Late Gooseberries.**—When gooseberries are past their first freshness, if a saltspoonful of ground ginger is added to the sugar for every quart of berries, it will take away the disagreeable tartness and improve the flavour.

1307.  **To Test Milk.**—If a polished needle be dipped into a deep vessel of milk and immediately withdrawn in an upright position, some of the fluid will hang to the needle if the milk be pure.

1308.  **To Prevent Beetroot Bleeding when Boiling.**— The broken roots can be sealed up by applying a red hot poker to the raw surface before the beetroot is put into the pot, or, if preferred, the end of the root can be thrust into the red hot fire and held  there for a moment.  Very long roots can be cut in two in this way, thus making it possible to boil them in the ordinary saucepan.

1309.  **When Gingerbeer has Gone Flat** and lost its sharpness, put a tablespoonful of sugar and a teaspoonful of rice in the bottle or jug.  Cork down tightly and shake well.  When opened it will be quite frothy and sharp.

1310.  **To Clean Bead Bags.**—Bead bags are difficult to clean owing to the dust in the crevices.  A good way of dislodging all the dirt is to rub the surface with crumbled new bread, which will prove even more effective when warmed.

1311.  **To Test the Purity of Flour,** grasp a handful and squeeze it for half-a-minute.  If pure it will preserve the form of the cavity of the hand.  If adulterated it will fall down.

1312.  **Clarifying Dripping.**—To clarify dripping, put into a basin, pour over it boiling water, and keep stirring the whole to wash away the impurities.  Let it stand to cool, when the water and dirty sediment will settle at the bottom of the basin.

1313.  **When Boiling Meat** keep the lid of the saucepan down tightly.  When boiling dumplings keep the lid of the saucepan raised.  If this is done the dumplings will never be heavy ; that is if the water is kept boiling the whole time.

1314.  **Care of Plants in the House.**—Do not put ferns or other house plants too near the fire in winter, or leave them in the full sun in summer.  Do not over-water them. They require to be kept just moist.  Do not let them remain in saucers full of water.  Do not keep them always in the same position.  Turn them occasionally, so that all parts of the plants can in rotation obtain the benefit of the light.  Cleansing of leaves : do not forget that plants breathe through their leaves.  You will help to keep an aspidistra in health by dusting its leaves.  Put the plants out in a warm shower.  Do not use very cold water when the room is warm.  The water should be at the same temperature as the room.  Tea leaves help to fertilise the soil and being entirely free from odour may be worked into the surface soil of room plants which need a little nourishment.

1315. **Another Use for Tea-leaves.**—Tea-leaves should be kept for sprinkling among the ashes when cleaning up a grate. It will be found that they allay the dust.

1316. **Concerning Ink Stains and Their Removal.**—When old, some kinds of ink stains are most stubborn and special means have to be employed to get rid of them, but when fresh they can usually be removed quite easily. For old ink stains : The surest and quickest way is to dissolve some oxalic acid in boiling water and immerse the stained part in the boiling solution, when the ink stain will speedily disappear. Ironmould will yield to the same treatment. But this is recommended only for white things, as the strong acid will remove the colour from coloured fabrics. Then again, when dealing with white silk or woollen articles the temperature must be considerably lower. In such cases after dissolving the oxalic acid the solution should be allowed to cool down until the finger can be borne in it, after which it is in a fit state to use. This solution is hot enough for ink-stained coloured things. In many cases Salts of Lemon will remove old ink stains, or it is only necessary to powder with salt the stained part and squeeze the juice of a lemon on it, and after leaving for ten or fifteen minutes, soap and rub the stain well and then boil. This treatment will usually remove a very stubborn stain. It is always advisable after treating ink-stain or ironmould to expose the part to the sun for some hours when this can be done. For fresh ink-stains much milder treatment can be adopted. Rub the wet ink mark with a ripe tomato and later rinse it with water. It is said that red ink applied over the black ink stain will dissolve the iron in the black ink, so that on washing, the stain vanishes but a trial I made did not convince me of its efficacy for removing an old ink stain. Milk, especially sour milk, is a ready means of getting rid of a fresh ink-stain. As the milk takes up the stain and darkens, rinse off and use more milk.

1317.  **A Bed-Warming Hint.**—While we are all aware of the advantages of having plenty of warm clothes on the bed in winter time, it does not occur to everyone to see that the bottom of the mattress is properly protected from the draught caused by cold air rising from the floor. Between the wool or hair mattress and the wire mattress it is advisable to place several layers of newspapers. The effect is surprising, as newspaper is a very bad conductor of heat or cold, and by its use not only is the warmth of the bed retained, but the cold, damp air from underneath is prevented from cooling the mattress. This will entirely prevent those rust marks which so often spoil the look of a mattress or its cover.

1318.  **To Shake a Doormat,** take outside and lay wrong side up on ground. Beat all over with wood side of the broom. This avoids strain of lifting and shaking, and also a disagreeable cloud of dust.

1319.  **An Excellent Method of Cooking Food** in the oven is to use two enamel pie dishes, same size, inverted over each other. This acts as casserole, fish kettle, bacon boiler, for stewed fruit, and saves cost of innumerable utensils. The combinations possible of boiling, steaming, and roasting are endless.

1320.  **To Cure Gnat Bites,** wet bandage in cold water, rub with preservene soap and apply—the irritation ceases like magic.

1321.  **To Sew Fine Materials like Crepe-de-chine** with sewing-machine, tack along seams strips of tissue paper, sew material and paper, tear off paper. This prevents cockling.

1322.  **To Clean Gramophone Records.**—You may clean records with a soft pad, but have you ever tried this way of freshening them. Make a lather with a little preservene soap and warm water, and wash gently and you will be surprised and delighted with the result.

1323. **Cooking—A Novel " Steamer."**—Fill the saucepan lid with potatoes, tie a cloth tightly over and return the lid. The potatoes will cook perfectly in this way, without any further attention.

1324. **To Clean Lacquered Goods,** or Papier Mache Articles.—Use a paste made with flour and olive oil. Apply with soft rag, rubbing vigorously. Wipe with another cloth and finally polish with an old silk handkerchief.

1325. **To Clean Rusty Curtain Rings and Pins.**—Cut up some preservene soap in shreds in a saucepan, adding a little common vinegar. Boil until the rings are clean. Take out, dry, and they will be found quite bright and equal to new.

1326. **To Clean Plush Curtains.**—Take a plateful of salt, dry it thoroughly, crush fine, then lay the curtains to be cleaned on the floor flat, after taking up the carpets for cleaning the room. Take a handful of dry salt, lay thickly on a piece of plush about a foot square. Rub that piece thoroughly with the flat hand the same way as the pile until the salt gets black. Treat all the curtains in the same way. Then take out of doors and thoroughly shake out the salt. After brushing they will look equal to new.

1327. **Rusty Black Lace.**—Soak lace for a while in vinegar and water (two tablespoonsful of vinegar to a pint of cold water). Rinse in cold coffee and iron whilst damp between flannel. It is wonderful how this treatment improves shabby lace.

1328. **To Remove Tracing Patterns from Fine White Embroidered Cloths.**—It is sometimes found on the completion of a fine piece of needlework that blue or yellow lines from the tracing pattern show near the embroidery. Spread the cloth on a clean table, carefully rub all the affected parts with preservene soap, moisten slightly with ammonia and then place across a bowl. Pour boiling water through and it will be found that the marks have all disappeared.

1329. **To Clean a White Sunshade.**—Make a good lather with hot water and preservene soap and dissolve a little pipeclay in it. Rub all over the sunshade well, and when dry, it will look like new.

1330. **Gilding on China.**—Never use soda for washing gilt china. Soda will in time remove it all. Instead of soda use a little preservene soap.

1331. **Instead of Ice.**—To hasten the setting of a jelly or blanc mange. Soak a cloth in a liquid made by mixing equal parts of methylated spirits and milk. Wrap this round the mould and set in a draught. A considerable degree of cold is produced by the evaporation. The characteristic odour of the methylated spirits is not noticeable when mixed with milk and therefore this extremely cold liquid will commend itself to the housewife for many purposes.

1332. **Cleaning Mackintoshes.**—Dip into cold water, then lay garment on the table. Make some strong preservene suds, have a soft brush, lightly scrub all over, lay it in the preservene water five or ten minutes, dip it in repeated waters. To get rid of the suds and dirt do not wring it : hang it up to drain, not near a fire (out of doors, if possible) or in an airy room.

1333. **New Brushes** should be soaked in cold water before using. Plunging them once a week into hot water to which preservene soap has been added, and hanging up head downwards to dry, will lengthen their life considerably.

1334. **Strings Sewn to the Corners of the Ironing Blanket** and sheet, and tied to the legs of the table will keep them from wrinkling during use.

1335. **Candle Ends** crushed small and placed in a pad of soft cloth will ensure the iron running smooth if occasionally passed over the pad. Should an iron be rusty, rubbing alternately with this pad and a cloth sprinkled with salt will put matters right.

1336. **Tussore and Shantung Silks** should be ironed dry or they will show patches where the damp has been.

1337. **A Carpet Hint.**—After sweeping with brush, bristles or vacuum, wipe over the carpet with a cloth wrung out of vinegar and water. Use one part vinegar and three parts boiling water. This freshens up the colour of the carpet tremendously.

1338. **Sateen.**—To retain gloss, wash with a lather of preservene and warm water. Into the rinsing water put a little borax. This is a splendid thing to gloss sateen.

1339. **Glass Ware and China.**—This should be washed in moderately hot water in which some preservene soap has been dissolved. Rinse in a bowl of clear warm water and dry ; then polish with a soft linen towel.

1340. **To Repair Iron Saucepans.**—Iron saucepans are dear and a crack or small hole spoils their usefulness. Here is a way for your good man to mend them. Buy some fine black lead and sulphur, put sulphur in an old iron pot ; place on stove to melt (use two parts of sulphur to one of blacklead). When sulphur is melted, add blacklead and mix gently. Then pour on an iron plate and leave to cool and harden. Break off a piece of this cement, put it on the cracked part of pan and solder with hot soldering iron. If a small hole in pan, put in a small copper rivet and solder well over inside and outside of the pan.

# ROUND THE SHOPS

## LABOUR-SAVING DEVICES FOR THE HOUSEWIFE

Manufacturers of to-day are fully alive to the importance and value of Domestic Labour Saving Devices.

As a proof of this, we have selected a few ingenious ideas which we recommend for the modern housewife.

**Knife Sharpener.**—For the small outlay of 3s. 9d. the housewife can purchase a British Made Knife Sharpener for either stainless or ordinary steel knives. The one we have in mind is fashioned on the old wheel principle and requires no oil or adjusting whatever. A useful addition to any home.

**Fork Cleaners.**—Every woman knows what a tedious job fork cleaning is, especially when one has to poke an ordinary duster down the prongs. All this labour, however, can be a thing of the past as, for about 2s. it is now possible to purchase a special leather fork cleaner. This device is constructed to clean all the prongs of a fork at once so that a few rubs and, hey presto, the job is done.

**Dustless Duster.**—An economical investment is a Dustless Duster which dusts, cleans and polishes furniture, metal or glass. This duster can be bought for the small sum of 3s. 3d. and retains its chemical properties after being washed and sterilized with hot water and soap.

**A Rubber Jug Mob** is a useful addition to the kitchen. It costs but a few pence and immediately and thoroughly scours all jugs and similar utensils.

**Vegetable Slicer.**—Only expert cooks can slice by hand cucumbers and similar vegetables thinly and evenly as they should be done. Housewives of to-day, however, can get for a few pence a patent vegetable slicer which does all this in a twinkling.

**Self Roaster.**—Five or six shillings to-day will buy a self-roaster—an absolute boon where an oven is not available.

**Self Toaster.**—No need to toast pieces of bread one by one. A wonderful little device can be bought for about 1s. which fits over an ordinary gas ring and toasts four pieces of bread at once.

**Rustless Expanding Curtain Rods.**—Neat and tidy curtains, without the worry and dirt of poles and rings. Rustless expanding curtain rods, which can be purchased at prices ranging from 6½d. to 2s. 11d. absolutely prevent sagging and cannot rust or injure the fabric. Actually these rods are fine closely made springs of rustless steel which fasten by being slightly stretched and hooked at the ends. The stretch or tension keeps them tight. These rods are, indeed, cheaper than ordinary curtain rods.

**Embroidery Needle.**—Embroidery which has hitherto been a long and tedious job can now be worked with a patent needle in the simplest possible way. Just poke the needle in and out of the material to be embroidered and the needle does the rest. Most stores sell this labour saver and the usual price is 2s. 6d.

**Rawlplugs.**—Every modern home will find the need and use of Rawlplugs indispensable. A household outfit costs 3s. 6d. and with its aid you can put up any fixture in any material in a few minutes. No special skill is required and once a shelf or rail is fixed with Rawlplugs it is always perfectly secure, no matter how thin or unsubstantial the wall may be.

**Kitchen Cabinets.**—Almost every American home possesses a kitchen cabinet. These are, of course rather costly. The prices ranging from about £12 to £25 according to make and size, but their usefulness is really wonderful. A kitchenette stores methodically every single thing for ordinary daily use. One which is extensively used in American homes has over forty work reducing features. Meals are prepared in less time. Clearing up after meals done quickly, and the entire cabinet can be taken apart and cleaned. A Kitchenette is indeed a step saving and comfort giving device.

**Dry Cleaning.**—Dry cleaning at home can be reallywell done with the aid of a new dry cleaning clothes brush now on the market. Its cost is 12s. 6d. The brush has a container for petrol, etc., inside the handle. In this way the cleansing fluid works down into the bristles as the clothes are brushed. A really ingenious labour-saver.

**Kettles.**—An improvement on the ordinary tin or copper kettle is one which is built to boil 4 pints of water in six minutes and whistles when the water reaches boiling point. These kettles save both time and money.

**Scrubbing Brush.**—A combined scrubbing brush and floor polisher for 5s. 6d. No kneeling at all ! These labour savers are hinged on the handle so that the action is identically the same as if the brush were in one's hand— but so very much easier to use in a standing position.

**Tin Opener.**—A tool which opens sardine and food tins like a pair of scissors. These handy little chaps cost 1s. 6d. and open any shape and thickness of tin. They also reject all metal filings and dirt and form a rounded-over edge which enables the contents to glide out of the tin entirely undamaged.

**Square Saucepans.**—The advantage of the modern square saucepan is that four saucepans can be economically fixed together over one ordinary gas ring and boiled at once. A square saucepan also pours out without waste and is a labour-saving investment.

**Frying Pan.**—The very latest has an asbestos lining. The prices range from 12s. 9d. upwards according to size and should prove a valuable acquisition for the kitchen. For instance this super frying pan will cook : fish in 2 mins., chip potatoes 3 mins., a steak 2 mins., a chicken 8 mins., a joint 12 mins, a fritter 1 min., and a jam tart 3 mins.

**Pudding Spoon.**—1s. will purchase a new pudding spoon with aluminium bowl. The advantages of this spoon are that it kneads or mixes puddings, cakes and pastry quickly and thoroughly and consequently makes them lighter. It also prevents waste as the shape of the blade enables bowls or pans to be scraped nearly clean. This spoon is strongly recommended for Yorkshire or batter puddings.

**Wash and Peel Potatoes.** Seven to ten pounds of old or new potatoes can be washed and peeled in three minutes without waste or stained fingers. This invention can be purchased for 12s. 6d. at most stores.

**A Magic Mop** for 6s. 6d. Quite the latest thing in floor mops is one which automatically twists and wrings out after the floor has been cleaned. Its daily use dispenses with all bending and even wetting the hands at all during the process of floor washing.

**An Addition to the Wardrobe.**—A new " garment fixture " will provide double the room in your wardrobe. They can be fastened to the under-rod of shelf or to the roof of a wardrobe. The fixture or " carrier " works on a special fibre roller that cannot possibly rust or stick. It makes room for seven extra hangers whilst the garments are kept at even distances from each other, so that any one can be removed without disturbing the rest. The prices range from 6s. 9d. to 8s. 3d.

**Lightning Mincer.**—Makes short work of chopping meat, pastry, herbs, etc. Also makes delicious strip salad. Cost 9d.

**A Novel Plate Squeegee.**—Plate and dish scraping is only one of the many uses for this scullery tool. It will remove grease from pots and pans with surprising rapidity. It will clean sinks and save many hours of hand rubbing. This Squeegee costs but a few pence.

**Pudding Basin Covers.**—One cover to fit all sizes of pudding basins. A patent pudding basin cover costing 5d. prevents scalding fingers, is no trouble to wash, saves hunting for string and has nothing to rust.

**Egg Separators.**—An efficient egg separator is a cheap and useful addition to any kitchen.

**Candles.**—The makers of a novel candle claim it burns 100 hours for a penny !

**Dry Cleaning Windows.**—An invention that will strongly appeal to housewives is the new window cleaning pad. This pad dispenses with water and makes the dream of dry-cleaned windows an accomplished fact. It can be had for the trifling cost of 6d.

**Electricity.**—There is scarcely one of the common tasks of the household that cannot be done far more conveniently and with greater cleanliness by the aid of electricity. Suppose you dispense with coal or gas fires ? Suppose you leave the oven to take care of itself, sure that whatever you are cooking will turn out well ? Suppose you arrange things so that your curtains only need washing once a year, instead of once every few weeks ? Suppose you do more washing and ironing in half the time ? And suppose you make everything more convenient without extra expense ? All these wonderful things, and many more, can be accomplished with the aid of electrical appliances in the Home.

**Rattling Windows.**—A very handy little window or door silencer is one that is instantly fitted and need never be removed. Windows glide up and down as smooth as ever. A whole set of four costs but 6d.

**Earthenware Egg Beaters.**—For beating eggs and whipping cream there is nothing better than an earthenware egg beater. A very useful size for the home costs, 2s.

**An Aluminium Spoon** with many points in its favour can be purchased at modern stores for 1s. 6d. The advantages claimed for this spoon are :—(1) Its broad surface makes it a splendid stirrer. (2) Its square edge thoroughly scrapes a pan, sides and bottom, no burnt stew on sides. (3) Peas, beans, potatoes, eggs, can be lifted out of the pan free from liquid, slightly tilt the spoon holes downward and the liquid runs out through the holes. (4) Liquid can be tasted without solid, tilt the spoon so that the holes are upward and you have a spoonful of liquor for tasting. (5) Unequalled for jam-making. (6) Separates the white from the yolk of an egg, place the spoon on a cup and break the egg in it. (7) Useful for scraping the pastry board. (8) A long hard wood handle, heat cannot reach the hand.

**Fly Swatter.**—A few pence will buy the very latest thing in "fly swatters." It is made of sanitary rubber on a wooden stick so there is nothing to rust. The makers claim that it cannot injure the finest furniture or fabric and it has the distinct advantage of being wholly washable.

**Shopping Indicater.**—There is no need to rely on one's memory for the daily household requirements. A very substantial indicator is now on the market for 2s. 5d. Made of white japanned steel it tells at a glance your requirements and daily needs.

**Fork Novelty.**—For serving fish, steaks, vegetables etc., for turning food either in a frying pan, on a grill or in the oven a novel two pronged fork is an efficient labour saver.   This fork costs to-day 1s. 9d.

**Strainer and Colander.**—Straining, mashing and pulping of all kinds can be done with the new style colander. It consists of a well-made steel body, removable straining and pressing mechanism and three different removable mesh wire strainers.   Average cost 6s.

**Collapsible Plate, Cup and Saucer Rack.**—No up-to-date labour saving scullery is complete without a plate rack of some kind.   Where space is limited, a rack of the collapsible variety is a boon.   They can be had for about 5s. 6d. from most stores.

**A Slate Meat Safe.**—Always stone cold and easily cleaned, the newest safes are made entirely of slate slabs, with polished doors and gauze.   These safes cost from 39s. to 149s., but they are, of course, built to last a lifetime.

**Clothes Boiler.**—An entirely new departure in clothes boilers is made of brown or blue enamelled ware out-side, and white inside.   It has a special double bottom which prevents the possibility of boiling dry and consequent burning of clothes.   The movable plate is fitted with holes through which the boiling water is forced, adding greatly to the efficiency of the boiler.   Average price 9s. 6d.

**A Scouring Mop** is much easier to use on a wooden handle, besides, it keeps the hands quite clean during the process of pot cleaning.   These can be purchased at general stores for 1s.

**Glass Jars for Use in the Larder.**—Absolutely air-tight jars with patent lids are now on the market and are an addition to any home.   Their use will keep away dampness and preserve the flavour of food of all kinds. Cost of 2 lb. size, 3s. 9d. ; 4 lb. size, 4s. 3d. The same patent lid can be had on fancy glass biscuit jars for 7s. 6d.

**Bath Painting Outfit.**—A novel idea is a complete bath painting outfit which is sold to-day for 6s. The contents include :—First coat bath enamel, finishing coat bath enamel, britton brush, bottle of thinning spirits, sandpaper, detailed printed instructions. It is claimed that the merest amateur can re-enamel a bath entirely satisfactorily.

**Whalebone Brooms** outlast at least two ordinary brooms. They are not more expensive to buy. Whalebone brooms have been in use for many years of course, but they are still the very best kind of broom. Whalebone, as most housewives know, is like no other substance in existence, natural or manufactured. Nothing else combines flexibility, resilience, strength and long wearing qualities to the same degree. That is why we recommend their use in the modern home. Whalebone is cut from what are known as " finners." These are slabs with hairlike " fringe," closely packed in the huge mouth of the whale who uses these as a sieve to catch the small creatures of the sea.

**Boiling Without Burning or Boiling Over.**—A cute little china device is now sold which, when placed in the bottom of a saucepan prevents burning or boiling over. Its cost is 1s.

**Sanitary Sink Cleaner.**—For speedily cleaning sinks a new rubber cleaner is sold for about 6d.

**Carpet Protectors.**—A set of four protectors costs 3s. These are similar in shape to the old glass piano feet. They are, however, made of wood and can be used for anything with a castor.

# THE PRESERVENE METHOD OF WASHING

## FOREWORD

THE advice and suggestions given in these pages are the outcome of many years of practical experience and observation. They are written in the hope that they may prove a useful and reliable guide and help to thousands of housewives.

It is an acknowledged fact that linen and clothes of all kinds are always a better colour when washed regularly at home. Women of to-day, however, are not anxious to stand all day over a wash-tub rubbing and scrubbing away at the clothes. They very rightly look for a quicker, cleaner and more scientific method. Indeed, rubbing and scrubbing the clothes on a wash-board with yellow soaps is not only hard on the fabric, but it is unhealthy, tiresome, wasteful and slow.

Therefore, these suggestions are presented to the housewife with the object of assisting her in her desire to get through her many household duties as quickly and efficiently as possible. By its careful study women will, in future, be able to devote the time saved through using the Preservene Solvent Method of Washing to other pursuit.

## TIME TABLE
### FOR A PRESERVENE WASH DAY

8.30    Half fill copper with clean, cold water. Shred up one bar of Preservene Soap and put into copper. Light copper fire.

        Shake out soiled linen and put—one by one—into the copper when the water is warm. Do not force too many clothes into the copper. Allow just sufficient for the water to work freely round the clothes and "draw out" the dirt.

9.30   The first copper or "boil" should now have had about fifteen minutes hard boiling. Rinse, wring and hang out.   Blue every other wash.

As in most homes one boil is insufficient, the second copper full will be ready again at about 10 o'clock.

10.30   Start washing woollens and coloured things.

11.30   Week's washing all finished and hung out.

## HOUSEHOLD LINEN

Soaking or "steeping" clothes overnight, whilst very useful when rubbing and scrubbing was the order of the wash day, is not necessary with the Preservene method of washing clothes.   Such articles as Sheets and Pillow Slips, Tablecloths and Napkins, Towels, Men's White Linen or Cotton Shirts, Children's White Underwear, etc., etc., all can be put straight into the copper from the soiled linen basket.

**Boiling.**—This is the first step in the Preservene method of washing.   Boiling water into which a bar of Preservene Soap has been shredded not only *draws out* the dirt, but purifies, sweetens and improves the colour of the clothes. *No soda, borax or other extract should be put into the copper unless the water is unusually hard.*

Place the soiled clothes into the copper when the water is only warm.   This will help Preservene to do its work. Let the clothes boil quickly for a quarter of an hour.

**Rinsing.**—The rinsing of clothes after boiling is very important. Lift the clothes out of the copper, carefully draining away the soapy water, and put them into a tub of clean, cold water.   Have the tub, if possible, placed under a tap of running water, and keep moving the clothes about until the soap is removed and the water on the clothes quite clean.

**Blueing.**—Preservene makes the clothes so white that the process of blueing is only necessary at every other wash. To prepare the blue-water, half-fill a tub with clean cold water. Dip the blue bag into the water and squeeze it tightly, repeating this until the water becomes a pale blue shade. Be careful not to make the water too blue as this will turn the clothes a pale blue instead of intensifying their whiteness.

**Handkerchiefs.**—These naturally require a little more attention than the ordinary articles. Place in a small zinc tub or basin together with a handful of common salt. Leave to soak for about thirty minutes. If not quite clear place in the sink and brush slightly before putting into the copper with the other clothes. Hot or cold water can be used.

**Kitchen Towels and Dusters.**—Pop these into the copper after everything else has been boiled and leave to boil for fifteen minutes.

**Wringing.**—It is usually advisable to put everything through the wringer before drying.

**Drying.**—Drying out of doors should, of course, be done whenever possible as the fresh air acts as a purifier and whitening agent. Hang all white clothes in the sun whenever possible. Sun rays kill germs. Hang shirts and nightgowns by the hem. Garments worn from the waist should be hung by the bands. This allows the water to drain from the thicker part and also keeps them a better shape. Dry all body linen on the wrong side. Hang handkerchiefs out in groups of three or four, pegging them by the corners. These are hung out to purify—drying is not necessary.

**Indoor Drying.**—A good method for those who live in small houses or flats is to hang the clothes on an ordinary drying screen in front of a bright fire. Drying on pulleys suspended from the ceiling is another method.

## WOOLLENS

The proper washing of woollen garments has always been a problem with the housewife. But after all, it only requires a little care and anyone can wash woollens without shrinking.

Wash woollens in lukewarm water. Make a soap lather by shredding Preservene into a proportion of boiling and cold water. Put the shredded Preservene into the boiling water and, when dissolved, add one and a half times as much cold water. This will bring the water up to just the right temperature. Simply squeeze the soapy lather into and out of the articles. Don't rub as this causes the fibres of the wool to entangle and the garment to shrink. Besides, it is not at all necessary with Preservene.

**Rinsing.**—It is a mistake to imagine that soap left in woollens keeps them soft and fluffy. As a matter of fact, even the best soap is liable to make wool stiff and felted. Rinse, therefore, with plenty of clean, warm water. The first water must be of the same temperature as the soap-lather.

**Wringing.**—It is very essential that woollens should be passed through a wringer. If this is not possible, twist as well as you can in a dry towel as woollens left wet too long are liable to get thick.

**Drying.**—Woollens need drying out-of-doors even more than linens, as the fresh air restores wool to its natural softness. If you *must* dry indoors, well shake and hang away from the fire.

**Woollen " tams."**—Stretch these over a dinner plate when washed. This will keep them in shape.

**Knitted Garments.**—As there are so many knitted jumpers, frocks and costumes worn nowadays, a word must be said about the best way to dry them. Follow method above for washing but before starting on the garment, that is to say, while it is still dry, lay it on a large piece of stiff white or brown paper. Pin it down, then carefully draw the outline with a pencil. After washing and partially drying with a towel lay it on the paper and stretch it to fit the outline of its original shape. Fix into position with pins and allow to dry. Dry on a lawn or in a shady part of the garden, or it can be laid flat on a carpet and left until dry.

SHAKE ALL WOOLLEN GARMENTS WHEN DRY.

## GENERAL HINTS

**Clothes Pegs and Clothes Lines,** if boiled for a few minutes in the copper after the clothes have been washed in the Preservene way, will last much longer. Always boil new lines in this way for ten minutes.

**Care of Wringer.** Oil wringer frequently. If oiled often there is less wear on the machinery and less strength is needed to wring the clothes. Always loosen rollers before putting wringer away. Wear rollers equally by wringing large articles in centre and small at each side. Fold buttons *inside* when mangling.

**Scorched Linen.**—If possible lay scorched article in strong sunlight. Sun rays will take scorch marks entirely out. Another method is to extract the juice from two peeled onions and add half ounce of shredded Preservene Soap and two ounces of Fullers Earth. Mix together, then stir in one cup of vinegar. Stand vessel over fire or gas and let contents boil up. When mixture is cool, spread over scorched linen and leave it to dry on the material. When well dried wash out the article.

**To Make Starch.**—To one quart of boiling water allow two heaped tablespoonfuls of starch. Mix smoothly with cold water, add a few drops of turpentine, and pour boiling water *straight from the kettle* until the starch is quite clear, stirring all the time. Stir for a few moments with a wax candle. This will help to make the ironing much easier.

**Cold Water Starch.**—To two heaped tablespoonfuls of starch allow a small teaspoonful of borax dissolved in boiling water. Add also a few drops of turpentine. Mix the starch to a smooth cream with cold water. Add the borax and turpentine.

**Ink Stains on Boards.**—Sprinkle liberally with salt and rub vigorously with half a lemon. Finally scrub with Preservene. Scrub up and down the grain of the wood—never across.

**To Clean Paint.**—Dust with dusting brush. Then make soap lather with Preservene and hot water. Rub lightly with a sponge. Dry thoroughly with a soft cloth. Wipe varnished or enamelled paint over with a damp washleather.

## DAINTY WEAR

Most silks, laces, chiffons, satins, muslins, etc., will wash successfully at home. The chief thing to remember when washing silk is to do this without twisting or displacing the fibres.

**Washing Silk.**—This is done by squeezing and pressing one part of the garment against the other in warm soap lather made with Preservene. Dirty marks and marks on the underarm part of blouse sleeves will quickly disappear this way. Rinse silk in plenty of clean water. A little salt may be used to fix colours that soften in the washing.

**Fine Lace.**—This must be treated with the greatest care. Make a soap lather with hot water and Preservene and shake in the lace. Leave for a few minutes and you will find all the dirt marks removed. Do not boil good lace unless you want it to look quite white.

**Tinting of Laces.**—Never use Ecru starch alone for tinting lace. The best results are obtained by mixing Ecru and white starch together. **Tinting with Tea.** Prepare a small quantity of tea and strain liquid from leaves. Tie a few pieces of hay of saffron into a piece of rag. Dip into the tea and squeeze until some of the saffron has dissolved. Tea without saffron may be used, but the tint is of a less delicate cream colour.

**Washing Chiffon and Georgette.**—Good quality Chiffon will wash many times with great care. Treat the washing process exactly as you would for fine lace and rinse in clean water. Stiffen with Gum-water—a tablespoonful to a quarter of a pint of water. Roll in a cloth to absorb some of the moisture, but it must not be too dry when ironed. Iron chiffon along the selvedge. Fold without pressing the folds in or, better still, roll it.

> *To make Gum-Water*—¼ lb. of cheap gum-arabic, 1 quart of boiling water. Wash the gum-arabic in cold water to remove the dust and wood fibre. Then add a quart of boiling water. Put in warm place and stir until the gum melts. Strain through a piece of muslin and bottle.

**To Wash Swan's Down.**—Washing is one of the cheapest and simplest methods for cleaning Swan's Down Fur. The following method will restore its new appearance in a remarkable manner. As the fur is very fine and easily destroyed, even squeezing in water must be avoided. Simply shake in a good lather of Preservene and, when clean, rinse in warm water and press to remove moisture. Shake to separate the down and hang in front of a fire to dry. Give it an occasional shake during the drying process.

**White Fur.**—This can be cleaned by rubbing gently with warm bran. Repeat the process until the fur is clean.

**Satin Slippers.**—To clean satin slippers brush all over to remove any dust. Pour a little petrol into two small basins, dip a small sponge into one and rub this gently over the slipper. When all dirt has been removed, squeeze the sponge very tightly, dip into the second basin, and go over the slipper once more. This is a kind of rinsing process. Place slippers in the open air to dry. When half dry, fill with soft tissue paper. This will help to keep their original shape.

## COLOURED CLOTHES

The more quickly coloured things are washed and dried the less likely are the colours to run. If you have the slightest fear of colours running, a good plan is to plunge the articles into salt water before washing and to rinse up in water to which common salt has been added.

**To wash Coloured Prints.**—Prints should be washed in a strong solution of Preservene soap lather. Sleeves and neck-bands, cuffs and fronts of shirts, children's overalls, etc., should be rubbed over with a little Preservene. This will draw out all the dirt no matter how soiled the article. Rinse in hot water.

**Brown Holland or Linen Dresses.**—As tussore-coloured linen becomes lighter in colour each time it is washed, it is advisable to take precautions, when washing it, to prevent the colour fading. It ought to be washed in almost cold soap lather. Make the soap lather with Preservene when the water is boiling and allow to get cool. Dry in the shade or indoors—not in extreme heat—and iron on wrong side, as linen, when new, has no gloss on the right side.

**Coloured Muslin.**—First prepare the soap lather with Preservene and let it stand until it is lukewarm. Squeeze in muslin until clean, then rinse thoroughly. Add a good handful of salt to the rinsing-water. Coloured muslin may be dried in the open air, but in a shaded place as sunshine would bleach the colours and entirely spoil the appearance of the garment. If it must be dried indoors, don't hang in front of the fire.

**Coloured Woollens and Flannels.**—These are washed in exactly the same way as white woollens and flannels, but because of the colour they must be quickly handled and only one at the time put into the water, especially if the shades of the colour are dark. The best way to preserve the colour is to steep or plunge into salt water and then wash quickly in cool Preservene soap lather. Rinse in slightly salt water, wring tightly.

**Stockings.**—This book would not be complete without a word regarding the correct washing of stockings and socks. It is a good plan to wash coloured stockings in the same lather after white or coloured flannels. Never rub stockings —especially silk ones—as this " ladders " the legs sooner than anything. If the feet are very dirty rub on a little Preservene and leave in the lather for about ten minutes. Turn on the wrong side and wring *across* the width to keep them in good shape. Shake well. Hang up by the toes. Black stockings are better when washed in a separate Preservene soap lather, otherwise they will show traces of white or coloured fibres, which adhere to them when washed in the same water as the woollens and flannels. Avoid sunshine drying in all black and coloured stockings.

**Black and Navy-Blue Serge and Tweeds.**—These can be washed and rinsed like all coloured woollens and flannels. If black or dark blue, they are improved if blued. It is well to choose a day when they can be dried out-of-doors as they are much improved if hung out without wringing. Finish by ironing.

## FURNISHING DRAPERIES

**Curtains.**—Curtains of any description, especially when near smoky towns, require fairly frequent cleaning. A large quantity of dust, however, can be easily removed by shaking, so whenever possible it is well to shake the curtains out-of-doors to remove the loose dust. Before washing curtains, steep them overnight in cold water into which a little soda has been added.

**Washing.**—White or cream curtains should be plunged into hot Preservene Soap lather and left out for about fifteen minutes. If very dirty, press and squeeze until they become quite clean. Rinse thoroughly in plenty of warm water and then in cold water. Never wring by twisting but pass quickly through the wringer.

**Cretonne,** when light in colour, is washed like ordinary print material.  After rinsing cretonne is best if slightly stiffened in a solution of equal proportions of boiling water starch and cold water.  Slightly dry and iron on the wrong side.

**Chintz and Holland Blinds.**—These can be treated exactly the same as ordinary casement or lace curtains, and must be stiffened in thick boiling water starch, to which a little melted Preservene Soap is added.  This gives softness to the material.  If a glossy surface is needed, a piece of white wax added to the starch will do this.  Partly dry blinds, etc., before ironing and iron on right side.

## MANGLING AND IRONING

**Points to remember when Mangling.**—Fold clothes evenly and in strips, with all hems at the ends.  The mangle must be quite free from dust as the damp clothes take up every speck of dust.  Turn handle of the machine slowly.  After being mangled, clothes must be aired as mangling, unlike ironing, does not dry the clothes.  In many cases mangling can take the place of ironing and thereby save endless time and cost of fuel.

**Hints on Ironing.**—Try standing on a soft thick rug.  This will prevent the feet becoming as tired as they otherwise would.

Irons must be absolutely clean.  A good plan is to run your irons on a little brick dust or sand.  Take great care that the *sides* of the irons are clean.

Pin your ironing blanket to the table.  This will prevent rucking or slipping.

Before ironing starched articles rub your iron with a duster in which odds and ends of candles have been placed. Your iron will then glide freely and smoothly.

To clean rusty irons, shred up a small piece of Preservene Soap into a little hot water.  Damp cloth thoroughly with the soapy solution and rub in a little bath brick.

The tops of worn out boots or shoes make excellent iron holders.

**To Iron Woollens.**—Woollen materials should not be touched with the iron at all. A piece of damp muslin should be laid between the iron and the material, to avoid that shiny look so ugly in materials of this description.

Start your ironing with the rough things first. The irons will work better after being used for a short time.

## BEAUTY HINTS FOR THE HOUSWIFE

A great drawback to housework from the housewife's point of view is its roughening effect on the hands, and the havoc played by dust and dirt on the hair and complexion. The actual exercise, however, is beneficial. The figure is developed and the muscles healthily exercised during such domestic tasks as washing, bedmaking and sweeping.

The prudent housewife takes a few simple precautions. For instance, a large overall, that completely envelops and protects the dress is essential. The woman who values the beauty and lustre of her " crowning glory " should wear a neat dusting cap. A good plan is to brush the hair well with an invigorating tonic every day.

**The Complexion.**—It is important to protect the face from dust. The best plan is to smear a little cold cream over the face and neck and wipe off with a soft handkerchief. Give a final dusting with oatmeal or any good face powder. This ensures full protection from dust. When the housework is over for the day, wash face in warm soft water and the face will be beautifully soft and fresh.

**The Hands.**—It is, however, the hands that suffer most on account of housework. The nails should be cut and filed fairly short. A little good cold cream should be rubbed freely into the hands or pure olive oil answers the same purpose. One of the best softening lotions for the hands is made by mixing equal parts of glycerine and rose-water and adding four or five drops of tincture of benzoin.

**The Feet.**—If the feet get very tired and aching, bathe them in warm water to which equal parts, a teaspoonful each, of alum, borax and sea salt have been added.

**Toilet Soaps.**—Always use the very purest of soaps for all toilet use. Preservene saves you the cost of bath or toilet soap. It contains ammonia, glycerine, borax, eucalyptus and coco-nut oil. It lasts much longer than ordinary toilet soap and does not waste.

# INDEX

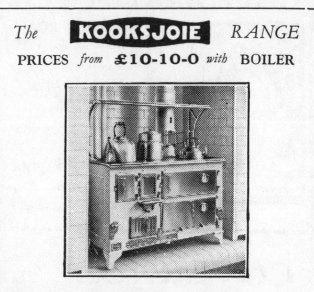

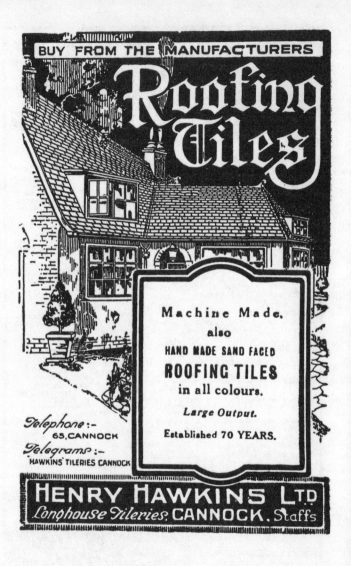